CULTURE, INC.

BY THE SAME AUTHOR

CULTURE, INC.

The Corporate Takeover of Public Expression

Herbert I. Schiller

OXFORD UNIVERSITY PRESS
New York   Oxford

To C. K. and W. K.

Oxford University Press

Oxford   New York   Toronto
Delhi   Bombay   Calcutta   Madras   Karachi
Petaling Jaya   Singapore   Hong Kong   Tokyo
Nairobi   Dar es Salaam   Cape Town
Melbourne   Auckland
and associated companies in
Berlin   Ibadan

First published in 1989 by Oxford University Press, Inc.,
200 Madison Avenue, New York, New York 10016

First issued as an Oxford University Press paperback, 1991

Oxford is a registered trademark of Oxford University Press

Library of Congress Cataloging-in-Publication Data
Schiller, Herbert I., 1919–
Culture, Inc. : the corporate takeover of public
expression.
Includes index.
1. Communication—Political aspects—United States.
2. Communication—Economic aspects—United States.
3. Corporations—United States.   4. United States—
Popular culture—History—20th century.   I. Title.
P95.82.U6S34   1989   302.2   88-36228
ISBN 0-19-505005-3
ISBN 0-19-506783-5 (PBK.)

2 4 6 8 10 9 7 5 3 1

Printed in the United States of America

Acknowledgments

Many individuals contributed to the writing of this book. Here, I mention only those to whom I am most directly indebted.

Sandy Dijkstra, good-humoredly but relentlessly, urged me to carry forward the project. Discussions with Bram Dijkstra about American art and literature of the 1930s and the disregard of most of that work over the last fifty years were invaluable. They supplied a necessary basing point from which to measure what has happened to public expression since then. Relatedly, Susan Davis's ideas and writing about the historical and contemporary treatment of public events and spectacles have been most helpful to my understanding of these phenomena.

Stuart Ewen, as in the past, was there when I needed him. Dee Dee Halleck, whose media efforts constitute a public sphere in their own right, sets the standard for my views on alternatives to commercially supported expression. I have been deeply influenced by Hans Haacke's works that strikingly reveal the (sometimes) hidden ties of art to power.

I thank Diane Neumaier for making available to me her exceptionally fine photographic record of the commercial envelopment of art sites and activities in New York City, headquarters of American corporate enterprise. Frank Webster continues to be a generous and reliable source of transatlantic informational-cultural developments. Carrie Menkel Meadow was an expert reader and critic of the chapter on corporate speech. Rick Maxwell offered valuable suggestions about current theories of media influence. Anita Schiller and Zach Schiller asked the right questions about the book's basic conceptualization. Dan Schiller was available for testing out one or another of my formulations. Eileen Mahoney, from the beginning, enthusiastically supported the work in progress while never abandoning her critical judgment. Her contribution to this enterprise is immeasurable. Rachel Toor read the first draft and made me re-think many of my statements. Scott Lenz edited the manuscript with care and sensitivity. I thank both of them. Finally, students in my communication senior seminar at UCSD in early 1988, gleefully tore into the draft chapters circulated among them for comments and criticism. Their willingness to challenge their instructor's written words, however deflating, also was heartening as an indication that critical thinking, despite eight years of Reaganism, survives.

La Jolla, California   H. I. S.
April 1989

Contents

Introduction

There have been eleven presidential elections since the end of the Second World War. The Democratic party has won its share, but the Republican party has done a bit better. National policies as well as specific programs have varied with the different administrations. Some of the swings have been considerable. The shift to the right in the two Reagan terms has been extraordinary.

Yet, however wide the policy differences and perspectives from one president to another, there has also been a basic continuity. And it is this para-electoral factor which has accounted for the essential features and direction of the times—far more, in fact, than the styles and programs of the various Democratic or Republican administrations. This deep and underlying element, long predating the Second World War but becoming more pronounced after it, has been the phenomenal growth and expanding influence of the private business corporation. Through all the political and social changes of the last fifty years, the private corporate sector in the American economy has widened its economic, political, and cultural role in domestic and international activities. Moreover, this consolidation of corporate power has taken place alongside a parallel decline in the influence of once important forces in American life—independent farmers, organized labor, and a strong urban consciousness.

The impact this expanded corporate power has had on the social landscape—especially the cultural activity and the visions that sustain a people—is the subject of this work. The drive to privatize and bring under corporate management as many elements of economic and social activity as possible in the last half century has tipped the balance of democratic existence to an uncomfortable precariousness.

This imbalance has much to do with the changed role of information in the economy.

A 1988 Office of Technology Assessment (OTA) study notes that "about 40% of all new investment in the United States now goes to purchase information technology—computers, telecommunication devices and the like. Just 10 years ago the share was only 20%."[1] The enormously expanded informational system that this technology supports and makes possible is directed and owned by a corporate handful. One consequence of the increased importance of information in a corporate-managed society is that corporate speech, advertising in particular, has been granted fundamental, First Amendment protection. The corporate voice, not surprisingly, is the loudest in the land. Institutions such as public libraries and the public educational system, which have provided free and open access to information and knowledge, are being brought into the corporate sphere, either through financial dependence or the transformation of information into a salable good. In either case, the erosion of equal access to information in the country progresses.

The sites where creative work is displayed—museums, theaters, performing-arts centers, etc.—have been captured by corporate sponsors. Such public events as street fairs, parades, and celebrations, too, have come under the same auspices. For most Americans, the daily transactions that living requires now are made in privately owned shopping malls, 30,000 of which are strewn across the land and constitute the current centers of shopping and commerce. However, these malls are privatized spaces, the uses of which are decided by the owners.

Meanwhile, the corporate-driven economy, impelled to expand or suffer contraction—there is no middle ground—has pushed beyond its national boundaries. The adventurers are the companies that operate in scores of foreign locales. This transnationalism of enterprise has brought to the world scene a comprehensive, corporate, informational-cultural apparatus which fills more and more national living space wherever it operates.

Curiously, these developments are treated by the currently dominant school of social analysis and cultural theory as hardly worth noticing. In the United States and England especially, the prevailing view is that the media, and by extension the entire information system, have little influence. Advertising, likewise, is seen as more ritualistic than effective.

Others, observing that the new information technologies routinely bypass national boundaries, conclude that the national state is no longer viable. What is not made clear is who or what is supposed to replace the national state. Though no one has suggested that transnational corporations should run the world (not even their executives), no other candidate has stepped forward. International organizations, to the extent that they are universalistic and allow each member state a voice, are deemed unworkable by the dominant forces that now govern the main Western nations. This is especially the situation in the United States.

The effects of these developments in the cultural-informational sphere at home and abroad are still to be fully experienced. But the prevailing outlook in the United States at this time is that there are no alternatives to the rules by which economic, political, and cultural affairs presently are ordered. Ways of organizing projects other than by private initiatives and reliance on market forces have been put beyond the boundaries of political consideration. This perspective is reinforced by the recent apparent eagerness of Soviet and Chinese leaders to adopt Western managerial, business, and media outlooks and methods. Consumerism, as it is propagated by the transnational corporate system and carried to the four corners of the world by the new information technologies, now seems triumphant.

In any case, it is evident that this is a period of great movement and change in economies around the world, one which will affect the destinies of people everywhere. It may seem, therefore, that the central theme of this book—the envelopment of informational and cultural space by the transnational corporate system—has been legitimized by recent U.S.–Soviet and U.S.–China accords.

Why question a social phenomenon if it appears to be the sought-after condition for the future by the world's major powers? Two reasons may be offered. First, it is by no means assured that the American model of the currently dominant informational-cultural system will become the global model of the twenty-first century. Though the world's social tectonic plates are shifting, their final resting place is still to be determined. The needs of billions of people for new institutional arrangements in resource allocation, state relations, and cultural sustenance may outweigh the political agreements that now seem to foretell the future. Whatever arrangements the long-term East-West rivals may conclude, the unmet needs of people in Africa, Asia, and Latin America assure the continuation and intensification of social struggles. Second, the developments in the United States have gone furthest along the road to corporate control. It is here that the outlines of a privatized, corporate-dominated society (though still far from completed) are most open to evaluation. What has transpired in America and what it may portend for the lives of Americans, therefore, cannot only be of interest to the United States.

I have looked mostly at the sweeping economic and technological forces influencing the institutional processes that, in turn, have set the direction of the postwar American informational-cultural enterprise. I have not intended to provide a framework for explaining the totality of human self-expression. There is, however, the strong assumption that social imperatives channel individual expression. These imperatives do exist, and some of them are outlined and examined in the chapters that follow. They do not lead to the conclusion that the substantive institutional changes that have occurred in the informational-cultural sphere preclude any kind of independent expression.

Individual expression occurs each time a person dresses, goes out for a walk, meets friends, converses, or does any of a thousand routine exercises. Expression is an inseparable part of life. It is ludicrous to imagine that individual expression can be completely managed and controlled. Yet, no matter how integral to the person, it is ultimately subject to social boundaries that are themselves changeable but always present. These limits have been created by the power formations in society, past and present. I have tried to trace how some of these defining conditions have been established or reinforced in recent decades and what impact they have. The growth of private corporate power is seen as the prime contractor in the construction of contemporary boundaries to expression.

The new technologies—at the service of corporate power—provide the instrumentation for organizing and channeling expression. This, in fact, is the connection—corporate power and the utilization of the new information technologies—that artist and critic John Berger calls attention to in his remembrance of Raymond Williams: "Modern technology is essential to the modern world. The danger is that the instantaneity of its techniques defines its aims. Instant greed. Instant prestige. The instant future. This is why a sense of history has become a condition for our survival."[2]

But modern technology has been designed, produced, and employed by the same corporations that have preempted national and international cultural and informational space. How to impart a sense of history when these commanding heights of social control are in corporate hands?

Consider, for example, former President Reagan's extraordinary references in 1987 and 1988 to the Abraham Lincoln Brigade. Reagan invoked the memory of those Americans who fought *against* Franco's counterrevolutionary troops in Spain in the 1930s. He did so to gain support for the "freedom fighters" his administration was underwriting in many parts of the world. U.S.–financed mercenaries, mobilized and paid by the CIA, have fought to destroy socially progressive regimes. The commitment made by the young American volunteers in the '30s was to protect a democratically elected government, attacked by forces that included Nazi and fascist legions.

Vicente Navarro, American health scientist, and in his youth a Spanish antifascist, comments on this astonishing but hardly unique ignorance in America that allows such mendacity:

> How remarkable, a brilliant and noble page of U.S. history has been stolen from the country's history books. And the makers of that history were and have since been persecuted. The feat, the eloquent feat of the International Brigades, well-known, admired and applauded not only in Spain but all over the world, was unknown and silenced in their own country. In Spain today, in the democratic Spain where the fascist nightmare has been broken, there are streets, squares, fountains and gardens named after the members of the Lincoln Brigade. In the United States, not one street, not one square, not one fountain is named after these veterans. . . . Why has that piece of history of which Americans should be so proud been stolen? Why?[3]

Paradoxically, the history-writing profession in the last twenty-five years has produced an outpouring of thoughtful and provocative works. These have excavated, reconstructed, and brought to light the aspirations, struggles, and achievements of the customarily disregarded but vast majority of Americans. A new generation of historians has supplied us with splendid accounts of another, noncorporate, America.

But while this exciting effort was being made, pitifully little—or nothing at all—of this important work appeared on the national media channels or in the historical allusions of the nation's leaders. There is, however, what can best be described as the corporate-sponsored, mass-media history machine. It churns out products that are processed and calibrated to corporate specifications. It provides national audiences with a historical view as seen from the top of the social pyramid. The corporate history machine has at its disposal the means by which it becomes the national narrator of record. Television, which takes its screening orders from corporate marketing, furnishes the history (such as it is) that is seen by the millions, be it through the news, drama, sports, or historical narratives. There is room for different interpretations of exactly how tens of thousands of writers, journalists, broadcasters, editors, and producers of videos and films are made to accede, or voluntarily shape their creations, to the taste of the Established Order.*

It is not necessary to construct a theory of intentional cultural control. In truth, the strength of the control process rests in its apparent absence. The desired systemic result is achieved ordinarily by a loose though effective institutional process. It utilizes the education of journalists and other media professionals, built-in penalties and rewards for doing what is expected, norms presented as objective rules, and the occasional but telling direct intrusion from above. The main lever is the internalization of values.

In the last forty years, the history machine has worked overtime. Not only have dissenters to the corporate model of America been dropped from the historical record. More perilous to the long-term national well-being has been the destruction of empathy and the erasure of identification with the less advantaged at home and abroad.

In recent decades, for example, the existence of significant unemployment has been made to appear as a normal part of national life. A newspaper report in 1986 noted that "For more than two years the nation's unemployment has hovered around 7 percent, a level long considered intolerably high and far above the 4 percent target set by Federal law. . . . Yet for all the lost production and individual distress associated with having 8.33 million Americans jobless—more than the population of New York City—a 7 percent unemployment rate seems to have become acceptable to the public, experts say."[4] It is indisputable that unemployment has not been a major political issue in recent years, despite its perseverance at a distressingly high level. The changing character of the postwar economy, the attrition of the organized labor force, and the values that have been generated by a temporarily triumphant corporate economy have enfeebled the

---

*A most illuminating account was supplied by the Writers Guild of America in testimony before a Senate subcommittee in 1971. In their statement, the writers, who at that time wrote all the network television dramatic, comedy, and variety programs produced in the country, declared: "It is our contention that the networks have deliberately and almost totally shut off [the] flow of ideas, have censored and continue to censor the writers who work for them" The Guild's account contained numerous examples of scripts altered by higher echelons. It also included a finding from a poll of its members that 86 percent of them "from personal experience," suffered censorship of their work.

once strong sense of social justice and solidarity that in an earlier time would have reacted strongly to this condition.

And so, approaching the twenty-first century, joblessness continues to afflict the work force. Electoral politics is meaningless to half the voters. National leaders and the governing elite honor conspiratorial war hawks and high-level influence peddlers. The media dutifully celebrate these charades and transmit them into the country's livingrooms.

In the midst of this debacle, workers and white-collar staff who are unable to escape it are treated to attitudinal training, underwritten by companies who are not content with the social atmosphere which is largely their responsibility. A *Wall Street Journal* report gives an account of one expression of corporate-sponsored consciousness massage:

> Abuzz with buzzwords, corporate America has started one of the most concerted efforts ever to change the attitudes and values of workers. Dozens of major U.S. companies—including Ford Motor Co., Proctor and Gamble, TRW, Inc., Polaroid Corp., and Pacific Telesis Group, Inc.—are spending millions of dollars on so-called New Age workshops. The training is designed to foster such feelings as team work, company loyalty, and self-esteem. . . . Most of the programs share a common, simple goal: to increase productivity by converting worker apathy into corporate allegiance.[5]

The reporter noted that not all of the participants, especially the older workers who had experience to draw upon, were enthusiastic about the training programs or the language, "New Agespeak," that went with them.

Variants of the new-age approach are numerous. At Stanford University's Graduate School of Business, for example, the syllabus for a seminar on "Creativity in Business," "includes meditation, chanting, dream work, the use of tarot cards and discussion of the 'New Age Capitalist.' " Further, "The Ford Motor Company, Westinghouse and Calvin Klein fashion house are among scores of major companies that have sent their employees for training to 'human potential' organizations . . . "[6]

What to make of these bizarre developments? Whatever the explanation or interpretation, the effect is that attention is diverted from the source of the problem—the corporate organization of society. The necessity for imagining and developing genuine social alternatives to the deepening crisis of the age is bypassed.

The self-promotional corporate canon on the "virtues of the market," recited by executives, government officials, and academics alike, permeates the national discourse and typifies the willful disregard for history. All the new-age language and seminars combined could not have produced a complimentary view of market forces in the depression years. But remembering the 1930s is dependent on history—history which is made available (meaningfully and clearly) and disseminated widely to the general public.

What follows is not a historical study. Its aim is to mark out, at least minimally, where the social order is at this time and how it has arrived there. It makes no claim on the future. If it provides even a few clues for future action, it will have been worth the effort.

| 1 |

Weakening the Democratic Order

The Second World War ended when two nuclear weapons were exploded successively over Hiroshima and Nagasaki. Many in the United States thought that this heralded a new age. Yet unlike atomic bombs, the forces that actually contributed to changing the lives of most Americans in the postwar period were not suddenly appearing, earth-shattering phenomena. They had been developing for decades. The war only speeded up the process.

The industrial power of the United States, for example, had been building steadily since before the Civil War. By the end of the First World War, America was becoming the match industrially of competing European states. But what had been a persistent, if unspectacular, incrementalism became a strikingly evident and tangible condition in 1945. The United States, all at once *it seemed,* was the global superpower, its factories and industrial plant the mainstay of what then remained of the world capitalist system.

Before this savagely destructive war, capitalism around the world had been stricken by economic crisis. The war dealt a still harsher blow to the Western industrialized nations and, no less, to the Japanese. Only the United States escaped the catastrophic losses of people, property, and industrial plant sustained in Europe and Asia. As shaken as its economy and business authority had been in the 1930s, the unique stimulus of the war to American industrial expansion brought to a culmination the process that had been under way for nearly a century. American capitalism had become the center of the international market economy.

Barely perceived, and even less well appreciated by most, was the new status of global controller of the world economy. But, in fact, for most people daily life was unaffected by the new world position so eagerly grasped by the nation's controllers. The distancing of most people from the full dimensions of the new reality uncoupled the country's overseas entanglements and interventions from domestic routines and individual lives and, less easy to understand, from the business system in general. The elevation of the authority of American business beyond the national to a world arena is one of the central features of global geopolitics of the last fifty years.

In 1981, the first year of the newly elected Reagan administration, the president addressed the annual meeting of the board of governors of the World Bank and the International Monetary Fund (IMF). The president explained how the world had been organized in 1945 for the postwar period. He said:

> The international political and economic institutions created after 1945 rested upon a belief that the key to national development and human progress is individual freedom, both political and economic.

Additionally:

> The Bretton Woods institutions and the GATT established generalized rules and procedures to facilitate individual enterprise and an open international trading and financial system.[1]

The "open international trading and financial system" is a reformulation of what has long been called the world-market economy. "Economic freedom" is a euphemism for private enterprise unfettered by social accountability. What the president was expressing more than a generation after the fact was that the world's economic rules, worked out in 1945 (largely under American auspices), coincided exactly with the objectives of U.S. corporate economic power—at that time, without competition.

There is nothing novel in identifying big business (corporate capital) as having been the main player in the domestic resource allocation process for at least a century or more. The story of determining who gets what in the United States has been told time and again, though it rarely becomes part of the textbook accounts of national life. As one writer recently put it: "The question of who owned financial wealth—or who did not—was the buried fault line of American politics."[2]

What *was* new in the postwar period was the greatly enhanced authority of American corporate business in deciding who would get what at the *global* resource table. The extension of governing power from a national to an international level, therefore, cannot be regarded as a routine, incremental change. It constituted a radical and qualitative transformation of the breadth and extent of power. Corporations also began displaying a strength and arrogance in the domestic sphere in this period that contrasted sharply with the preceding period of economic depression.

But much more was involved than renewed confidence—a rather elusive and subjective condition at best. The tribute derived from global resource-allocation control—what empire actually is all about— enabled big business to gain the support of the general population, in particular, the domestic work force for the new American expansionist policy abroad. Passing down to labor—at least to organized labor—a small portion of the tributary flow derived from being number one globally, U.S. business for twenty-five years had no need to look over its shoulder and reassure itself that the public, and especially the work force, was in tow. It was.

Postwar Dominance of Big Business

The greatest part of the booty stayed in corporate hands. Here it fueled the rapid expansion of already huge enterprises, enabling the capital-rich companies to establish operations and branches around the world and thereby to tighten their grip on international production, trade, and finance. In twenty years, privately owned U.S. production facilities were built or acquired in scores of countries. To assist these enterprises, U.S. banks set up shop in the new locales—so did American advertising agencies and public relations and marketing firms. A global infrastructure of American-owned production, marketing, distribution, and finance was created in an astonishingly short time.

Though many elements in this new, global, private economy were visible, the inner workings of the system often eluded governmental administrative control, to say nothing of being a total mystery to the population at large. What in fact was a privately administered world order outside the known international structures (such as the United Nations and its affiliated bodies) became the site of major resource decisions on production, investment, industrial policy, finance, and media activity, affecting people in a large part of the world.

The consolidation of the power of big business was accomplished in a number of ways. Sometimes corporate initiatives were taken. In

other instances, technological and social developments worked toward the same end. Some of the contributing factors were:

- the use of anticommunism to control labor as well as to divert the
  general public from the expansionist policy of American business
- the adoption of new farm technologies which increased output at
  the same time as it eliminated a good part of the independent farm
  population
- the influx of a conservative immigrant stream
- the spread of depoliticized living space, i.e., suburbanization
- twenty years of relative prosperity and "good times."

These and other factors allowed business to pursue its objective of
organizing the world economy to suit itself almost undisturbed. In
securing the acquiescence of the general public for this goal, the
instrument of anticommunism was especially effective. The fear that
communism generated was bound up with the population's deep desire for postwar stability and prosperity.

Actually, "anticommunism" had a long and nasty record in American history. The same spirit was expressed decades *before* the Russian
Revolution under a variety of labels. Campaigns and vigilantism were
undertaken against those who were called "anarchists," "aliens," "ter-
rorists," and, of course, "communists." Invariably, these were individuals active in protesting one or another of the exploitative practices
of the propertied and governing class. An editorial, for example, in
Harper's Weekly in 1874 could have been written anytime in the last
forty-five years. It read:

> [The] cartoon on our front page sets one phase of the labor question in a
> very clear light, and will serve to warn reflecting working-men against
> some of the dangers upon which misguiding leaders may precipitate
> them. . . . Communism is a foreign product, which can hardly be made
> to flourish on American soil.[3]

The Russian Revolution, however, and its Bolshevik denouement
in particular, made anticommunism a permanent feature of the
American landscape, a tactic to be resorted to whenever unusual
stress or strain troubled the tranquillity of the established social order. The Russian Revolution itself invoked an orgy of vituperation
and fear in the country's affluent strata, fed by the alarmist exaggera-
tions and distortions of the American press.[4]

Periodic eruptions of anticommunism have footnoted the last seventy years. In 1920, in the aftermath of World War I, worker demands for jobs and security, coming in the wake of the upheaval in Russia, created apprehension in the middle class. The response was the Palmer Raids in 1920, directed against aliens and alleged "subversives," in which thousands of people were arrested.[5]

Throughout the depression years, protests against unemployment, plant shutdowns, and farm foreclosures precipitated intermittent upsurges of anticommunist sentiment and attacks on cultural and intellectual workers in the theater and in the classroom. Although the decade of the 1930s is known for the social legislation enacted—the New Deal—it is also the time of the creation of the Congressional Committee on Un-American Activities. Under its chair, Martin Dies, the committee became synonymous with anticommunist witch-hunts.[6]

In the 1940s, what had been a recurrent phenomenon became a continuing, never-absent feature of American life. Postwar anticommunism differed from the earlier species in that it did not subside. It was legislated into daily life and institutionalized with vaguely drawn legislative measures, which, in effect, made ideas as well as political affiliation illegal. The Smith-Mundt (1948) and McCarran-Walter (1952) acts, the Taft-Hartley labor law (1947), and other pieces of legislation[7] made affiliation with the Communist party and other allegedly related organizations sufficient cause for exclusion from government jobs and many other kinds of work, as well as cause for legal prosecution. A pariah status was created for those accused of deviant political views. Social criticism of all varieties was suspect and, consequently, increasingly muted.

Another departure from earlier "anticommunist" eras was that after the late '40s and early '50s "McCarthyism," the anticommunist fever, broke out in response to what was identified as an *external* crisis. Not at all as evident as it is today, the external threat then—if that term is justified at all—was (is) the possibility that significant chunks of the excolonial world might break away from the world business system, adopting some form of socialist economy. This possibility was transmuted by the governing class and its enthusiastic accomplices, the media, into the "Soviet threat." Accordingly, those who continued to believe that cooperation and peaceful interaction between the United States and the Soviet Union and the People's Republic of China were possible and desirable were the domestic targets of the anti-red campaigns—so were those who continued to defend uncompromisingly labor and consumer interests, in the largest sense, against the world-dominant American corporate leadership.

Yet anticommunism, defined explicitly as "anti-Sovietism," was no inexplicable, irrational phenomenon. It was a sophisticated policy—at least at the highest levels—formulated to satisfy many of the most urgent requirements of the world-expansive American enterprise system. As with all such political efforts, it is important to distinguish between the actual beneficiaries of the policy and its mass cheering section, which, at best, gains only psychic satisfaction.

Who, then, were the beneficiaries of the fabricated Soviet "threat"? They included the newly established global interests of U.S. corporate business which received "protection" from a worldwide network of American military bases deployed to counter "potential Soviet aggression." At the same time, the military theatrics diverted attention from what was actually happening on the global central stage—U.S. economic, political, and cultural expansionism. Instead, increased Soviet control over Eastern Europe (of no significant strategic importance) received the media spotlight.

There were additional, substantial benefits from the anticommunist tumult. A huge protected market for American industrial production was created. The vast military shopping list, underwritten by unstinting congressional appropriations, meant that aircraft, shipbuilding, electrical equipment, automotive, and, most consequentially for the long-term, the new information industries had a ready buyer: the Pentagon. The new information technologies—computers, satellites, and a growing number of electronic marvels—owed their existence to military interest and support.[8] This high-technology sector became the main hope of achieving ultimate military superiority over the Russians and providing an edge to the American economy, hopefully enabling it to maintain a global position of authority into the twenty-first century.

Less substantively, but of ideological interest, the new developments in electronics and communication stimulated an outpouring of "futurist" writing, which endowed the new instrumentation with far-reaching social utility—ignoring the fact that most of the new technologies were designed specifically for coercion, social control, destruction, and death.

Perhaps the most significant effect of the protracted anticommunism of the postwar period is invisible and immeasurable. It is embodied in the muddled debate, the absence of a genuine spectrum of public opinion and expression, a popular culture saturated with political propaganda, and a numbing acceptance of a political environment in which the president of the United States tells anti-Soviet jokes.

A year *before* the election of Ronald Reagan, Leslie Gelb, a former director of the Bureau of Politico-Military Affairs of the State Department and a longtime political correspondent for the *New York Times,* wrote a short piece entitled, "The Death of the Center." In it he reflected:

> The political center that used to provide the ballast for United States foreign policy is just about destroyed and is being replaced by the right wing. . . . With few comprehending what has been happening, the right is beginning to take over the political middle ground, the ultimate test of success in American politics.

Gelb concluded:

> Unless moderates and progressives respond to this way of "thinking" and realize they are in a battle, the right wing will become the center and its cut-throat politics and the frightening logic of its policies will pass for common sense.[9]

What Gelb chose not to mention was that the elimination of the left thirty years earlier had paved the way for the demolition he was lamenting in the late '70s. However, during the Reagan years, it was not only U.S. foreign policy that was taken over by the right wing. The entire political-cultural spectrum had shifted as well.

Organizations, groups, and individuals who constituted the fringe right in the immediate postwar years have moved into the center of respectability. They now dominate the columns and airtime of the mainstream media. It is not that conservative thought and expression were absent from establishment opinion-making in earlier years. Rather it is the near preemption of informational and cultural space by that perspective in the 1980s.

How deep the conditioning has gone is indicated in a survey conducted in 1987 by the Gallup organization for the Times Mirror Company, one of the nation's largest media combines. Polls, to be sure, are notoriously manipulable, often providing confirmation for what the pollster, or the sponsor of the pollster, wants to hear. All the same, they can be revealing. In this survey, the subjects were asked to identify themselves by selecting the one classification of many listed that best described their outlook. Seventy percent of the respondents identified themselves as anticommunist. No other category came close. Next in order was "Religious" with 49 percent, followed by

"Supporter of Civil-Rights Movement" with 47 percent. The full table lists these categories:[10]

Anti-communist	70%
Religious	49
Supporter of Civil-Rights Movement	47
Supporter of Peace Movement	46
Environmentalist	39
Supporter of anti-abortion movement	32
Democrat	31
Feminist, supporter of women's movement	29
Supporter of business interests	28
Conservative	27
National Rifle Assoc. Supporter	27
Union supporter	27
Pro-Israel	25
Republican	20
Liberal	19
Supporter of gay-rights movement	8

The steady inculcation of anticommunist sentiment into the population has permitted a shocking number of national acts of violence to be committed. How else to describe the state-directed, systematic murder—U.S. military interventions since 1945—carried on in the name of fighting communism? Enormous losses of human life have been suffered in Korea, Greece, the Dominican Republic, Lebanon, Cuba, Vietnam, Grenada, Nicaragua, El Salvador, and elsewhere following American armed actions or support for mercenaries (as in Angola, Mozambique, etc.). "Better dead than [possibly] Red" has been the operational principle of U.S. foreign policy for half a century.

The impact of anticommunism on American culture and consciousness, if less deadly, has been no less destructive. The "death of the center," one consequence of the unremitting anticommunism, also made the triumph of corporate perspectives and values realizable in the postwar period.

Big Business: The Only Viable Alternative

Once socialism—linked to the dread communist threat—has been made an unthinkable project, the most minimal social reforms can be presented as dangerous. "Strict constructionists" of the market model found that any interference with private ownership and enterprise was a perilous step toward concentration camps. Even the most venerable public institutions (e.g., the postal service and the weather bureau) in recent years have been viewed from this perspective as unattractive embodiments of statism, inefficient at best and better administered by private enterprise.

Starting from this point, it was a small step to the notion that the public's choice in modern society is between big government and big business. Leaving aside the collapsed character of such a "choice," putting big business and big government as paired equivalents is in itself an ideological construct that privileges big business.

Big business today is the locus of systemic power. It is the site of the concentrated accumulation of the productive equipment, the technological expertise, the marketing apparatus, the financial resources, and the managerial know-how. It is a tangible reality, not a metaphor. Moreover, the interests of big business are most powerful in the formulation of national and international policy.

Contrariwise, "big government" is a term originated and used pejoratively by the "big media"—the strongest defenders of the corporate system—to weaken accountability and responsibility of representative government. The propositions that the choice is between big government or big business and that in the final measure business is less threatening than government disregard the basic interests of the vast majority of people.

Large-scale government agencies do exist, and bureaucratic policies are not unknown. Yet it is not these features that account for the negativism in the corporate media against what they call big government. When abuses are discovered in the practices of the largest government bureaucracies (the military, the semi- and fully secret intelligence agencies, and the investigatory services like the FBI and the Treasury)—and these occur relatively often—the media are compelled to comment on them. But their disapproval generally is mild and rarely, if ever, involves recommendations for curtailing the size and budget of the offending unit.

The agencies that usually incur the displeasure of the corporate class and its mass media are the *social* units of the government—social security, health, education, agricultural assistance, environmental protection, occupational health and safety, et al. Whatever their failures, there is little doubt that these agencies are warmly supported by the public. In fact, it is the desperate need to expand the functions and activities of these agencies and to make them more responsive to the public that constitutes an agenda for political action in the years ahead. Thus, it is the *social* component of "big" government that remains the protection of last resort for most people. The *coercive* agencies of big government are the instrumentalities by which privilege maintains its grip on the social order.

In the political atmosphere that has been created in the postwar years (reaching its apogee in the Reagan period, 1980–88), the threat of "big" government has served well in disarming criticism of private, concentrated economic power, which has grown to formidable levels. The continued alarms, generated by the power centers of the national administrative apparatus, have facilitated the growth of the national security state. Gigantic military expenditures over the decades have fostered the creation of a core of industrial power heavily dependent on military orders. The work force of this protected enclave, no less than its managers and shareholders, finds the military-corporate definitions of national security and geopolitical strategy supportive of continued employment, executive perks, and shareholder profits.[11]

Over time, the military-industrial complex has been extended to the academic and scientific communities as well.[12] Military and corporate support underwrite a significant and growing fraction of university research. In the 1980s, this almost all-encompassing web defines social reality in the classroom, in the media, in professional life, and in the nation at large. A great part of the huge message and image flow that circulates is originated in this complex in one way or another. Those outside this powerful interlocking network of resources and influence find it exceedingly difficult to obtain a channel of expression that can reach a national audience.

While large-scale corporate enterprise has become the dominant, near-exclusive mode of national production and distribution in the postwar years, the anticommunism that saturated the national dialogue insured that criticism of this development would be well-contained within acceptable, private-enterprise assumptions. When some especially egregious corporate act, for example, could not be overlooked by the media, it could be attributed to an individual miscreant or a temporary lapse in executive judgment in one enterprise. The "one bad apple" explanation generally served to extricate the *system* from scrutiny and responsibility.

At the same time, structural changes were occurring that not only were remaking the economy, but which also were contributing to a further weakening of what were once substantial independent sectors—sectors which supported significant numbers of people who were able to retain and exercise some vestige of independent thinking. The decline of those sectors gave the corporate voice still greater opportunity to dominate the national arena.*

If the American frontier came to an end in the 1890s, agriculture as a sizable sector of independent farms and farmers all but disappeared by the 1980s. By 1985, only 2.2 million active farms remained in the United States, a precipitous decline from the turn of the century when agriculture still accounted for over 30 percent of the population. As late as 1945, at war's end, nearly 6 million farms were being worked in the country.[13] By the mid-1980s, not only had the number of farms declined drastically but also most of those that remained—at least the big ones—had been "corporatized." It was reported in the *New York Times* that "currently the 200,000 biggest farms produce roughly 60 percent of the nation's food," and that they "earn more than half of all farm profits."[14] The expectation is for still more concentration and further growth of corporate-owned farms as the new biotechnologies begin to be applied. The cost of using the genetic engineering technologies and products is most assumable by the already extensive farms. Application of these new techniques will increase further the gap between the big and small farms, with many of the still remaining weaker units unable to continue.[15]

The transformation of the American economy from agriculture to industry and now to the new, science-based information technologies has been a long-term movement. Its effect on the character and tone of the social order is not easy to assess. Yet the near elimination of small-scale, family-farm agriculture in the United States has an influence on the democratic texture of American life that goes beyond strictly economic factors. It has meant the exodus of millions of people who at one time—though dependent on the market, bank credit, and other imperatives of a capitalist economy—lived *relatively* autonomous lives. This once-large component in American society now barely exists.

---

*Alternative developments could be identified that would present a "positive" picture of postwar America—the explosion in higher education, for example, where today there are eight million college and university students compared with scarcely a million in prewar days. Another seemingly heartening indication is the gigantic growth in popular appreciation—as measured in attendance—of cultural activities (museums, galleries, concerts, etc.). Yet it is precisely these apparently hopeful indications of social improvement and maturity that need to be examined and questioned. It is in these areas that the corporate influence is most visible. Accordingly, rather than cheerily quoting statistics of the number of PhDs granted, college degrees conferred, and the attendance at museums and concerts as empirical measures of an American cultural renaissance, the focus in this work is on what lies behind this undeniably active cultural scene.

It is not necessary to romanticize the agricultural population as a redoubt of rugged independence, representing a center of democratic values, uncontaminated by city vice. Still, it is not farfetched to view it, conservative as it generally was, as a source of independent thinking. At least in the late nineteenth and early twentieth centuries, agriculture produced serious opposition to the country's already dominant forces of concentrated wealth and finance. Today, active and nationally significant farm protest is absent from American life. Whatever strength remains in the agricultural sector is wielded by corporate farms and agribusinesses. Their outlook and interests, on the larger political issues, are indistinguishable from those of the dominant corporate industrial sector. In sum, since the end of the Second World War, one important social pillar, not in the corporate orbit, has been almost completely demolished. Nothing comparable has replaced it.

While the independent farmer has been the victim of world-market forces and domestic, large-scale corporate agriculture, organized labor has faced a different but equally damaging onslaught in the post-war decades. Powerful opposition to working-class demands is no recent phenomenon in American economic development. Historically, the labor movement in America has had to fight bitterly for whatever improvements in work and life it could wrest from employers. American capitalists, unlike their counterparts in other industrialized countries, successfully resisted unionization in the heavy industries until little more than half a century ago.

Largely on account of this continuing struggle by working people to improve their lot, the objective of democratic social change has been an inseparable part of the labor movement's history. Efforts against child labor, for a shorter work week, against discriminatory treatment of women, for expanded education, and, most important of all, for participatory rights in the work place contributed to democratic practices in the economy and to placing democratic goals on the national political agenda. Without suggesting virtuous intent, the labor movement's demands and efforts have been a core component of the general struggle, waged since the earliest days of the country, for meaningful democracy. These included the rights of the many to enjoy economic as well as political representation in national decision-making. If what was beneficial to labor was good for the country, the nation has suffered grievously in recent years.

Union membership is a significant measure of the strength and well-being of the labor movement's general condition. Using this measure as a rough guide, the high point of union membership, as a percentage of employees in nonagricultural jobs, was reached at war's end, when it peaked at 35.5 percent (by no means as high, even at its peak, as what could be found in other industrialized, capitalist countries—Great Britain and Australia, for instance). In 1984, however, the percentage of union membership was calculated as 18.8 percent. "Only 14 percent of all private nonagricultural wage and salaried workers were organized."[16] This overstates the decline because union-organized employees have increased in the public sector. Yet in the new industries, especially information and high technology, unions have been almost totally excluded. In the major manufacturing industries where union strength formerly was greatest, plant shutdowns and industrial cutbacks are most marked.

Yet the numerical shrinkage of organized labor, as well as its reduced importance as a support of democratic social life, began well before the onset of the world economic slowdown in the late 1970s. The latter only further accelerated the downward course already observable. When and why did this decline begin? At the end of the war, labor was stronger and better organized than it had ever been. In 1946, for example, immediately after the demobilization of the armed forces, a number of major strikes were militantly and successfully undertaken.

At the same time, however, American business was preparing to begin its global march forward. For this to be successful, management realized that a reliable domestic base had to be guaranteed. This translated into a work force that would not be troublesome, economically or politically. To achieve this end, a rationale had to be formulated that would justify American capital's worldwide expansion. This was provided by anticommunism in particular.

The rediscovery of the Russian menace put a gloss on overseas activity that otherwise might have been seriously challenged at home. The alleged "communist threat" was especially helpful in gaining the neutralization and more often the active support of organized labor's leadership for an American foreign policy of global expansion. An early instance of this use of anticommunism was during the civil war in Greece. In 1947, the British Empire no longer had the resources to maintain its privileged position in that country against the indigenous, communist-led partisans who had liberated a great part of the national territory from the Nazis. Under the banner of the Truman Doctrine, the United States took over custodianship of Greece, supplying troops, arms, and an open checkbook to defeat the Greek resistance movement. American bases were established—which remain to this day. For thirty years, Greece has provided a secure Southern Mediterranean flank to U.S. interests in Southern Europe and the Middle East.

The Truman Doctrine and the intervention in Greece, explained to the American public as a necessary move in the containment of communism, received approval and support.[17] This rationale not only misrepresented what was happening internationally, but it also provided the means by which the unions could be "sanitized." Instead of irksome critics, they could be transformed into ardent champions of the deepening American involvements abroad. And so, well before Senator Joseph McCarthy arrived on the scene to purge the State Department, the universities, and—not so successfully—the army, similar tactics had been applied successfully against organized labor.

Leaders of many of the major unions long had been anticommunist. The rapidly emerging Cold War situation from 1945 on enabled them to move against their adversaries with full support from other power centers in the country. The leaders of the automobile, steel, transport, maritime, and other key unions carried out purges against their communist officers and members. Other important unions, either voluntarily or under government-employer pressure, applied the anticommunist provisions of the 1947 Taft-Hartley Act. This law, along with other demands, carried the requirement that all union officials sign affidavits affirming that they were not members of the Communist party. With this stipulation, the targeted leaders were put into an intolerable double bind. If they refused to sign the affidavits, their unions lost essential government protection against employer practices. If they complied and signed, it was all too likely that they would be prosecuted for perjury on the testimony of government-supplied informers. In either case, the individual unions and the labor movement in general were weakened.

By the early 1950s, most, though not all, of the trade unions, by one means or another, had ousted from their ranks members and leaders who challenged U.S. foreign policy. No less significantly, gone as well were those who had represented firmly the interests of labor against capital.[18] Once these ousters had been achieved, the organized component of the labor movement ceased being a serious source of concern to corporate management. Acquiescent, if not celebratory, to one U.S. military interventionist act after another, the union movement reached its nadir when the majority of its leaders gave near-unqualified endorsement to the U.S. war against Vietnam.

Anticommunism set the parameters of discussion and policy: larger issues of the social order could hardly be expected to receive critical attention, much less organized action. Thus, the management of the economy, the goals of production—basic needs, for example, versus upper income luxury goods—the safeguarding of the environment, the use of nuclear energy, public versus private sector interests, etc., received short shrift. With serious consideration of the social economy abandoned, unions busied themselves with what was left—short-term issues, not unimportant, but separated from the wider and more fundamental framework of social existence. As long as the expansionist policies succeeded and international markets remained open and clamored for American goods, organized labor managed adequately within the narrow boundaries it had accepted.

When the political and economic tide turned after the defeat in Vietnam and the international economic boom subsided, organized labor was without direction and unable to resist its rapidly eroding situation. To maintain profit margins, U.S. transnational companies shifted production to their branch plants in low-wage locales. Older industries closed down or cut back harshly. Yet after foregoing political action for decades, holding to the most immediate and narrowest economic issues, supporting the transnationalization of business, becoming literally a (very) junior member of the power coalition that governed the country since 1945, unionized labor found no allies when the American global supremacy came to an end. Labor's corporate business "partners" savagely cut wages, laid workers off, speeded up the work pace, and demanded "give backs" of gains that had been won over half a century.

The rest of the working population, the unorganized majority, having witnessed the selfishness, the greed, the limited social perspectives of most unionized labor, felt little inclination to give support to unionization when the antilabor onslaught accelerated in the Reagan years. In the late 1980s, even the long-revered principle of labor solidarity hardly survives. A report in the *New York Times* states that "while many workers might once have considered it unethical to cross picket lines, that no longer seems to be true." Another observer claims: "scab doesn't have the same meaning it had in Detroit in the 1930's and 1940's."[19] Though these judgments may in part represent reporters' too ready acceptance of employers' wishful thinking, they cannot be dismissed.

As unions lose power both internally and in terms of their ability to attract workers, an even more calamitous problem is the disappearance of labor's voice in the national dialogue. A voice that was formerly influential in agenda setting, that could be offering alternatives to the deepening socioeconomic crisis and to the political miasma that engulfs the nation, now is, in fact, practically inaudible.

The Impact of Postwar Immigration, Suburbanization, and Prosperity

Another structural development in postwar America, assuredly not of the same magnitude as the weakening of labor's influence but still affecting the country's democratic fiber, has been the heavy immigration throughout the period and especially in recent years. The 1980 census revealed that "the size of the foreign-born population of the United States had not only reversed its 50-year downward decline but had sustained a quantum increase. As a group, the reported foreign-born population rose from 9.6 million in 1970 to 13.9 million persons in 1980 (an increase of 45%). . . . Given the momentous immigration movements since 1980, the foreign-born population to be recorded by the 1990 census will show another quantum leap."[20] And, in fact, the Center for Immigration Studies concluded that the number of legal immigrants in the 1981–90 decade will surpass the hitherto record flow that came into the country in the 1901–10 period.[21]

What is the relevance of this upsurge in immigration to the current state of American democracy? Until World War II, immigration constituted a major source of population growth in the country. And despite periodic nativist attacks on "foreigners"—one of the targets in the 1920 Palmer Raids, for example—the immigrants added a fresh and vigorous input to domestic political and social life, joining readily in liberal protest and social-reform movements. The Europeans, along with seeking economic opportunity, came, in large measure, to escape repressive political conditions and to enjoy the relative openness of the American political environment and its promise of democracy.

To what extent this characterizes recent immigration is quite another story. Time and again over the last forty years, the incoming migrants have been leaving countries where there have been revolutions whose changes apparently were unacceptable to those departing. First, there were the East European outflows in the early postwar years, then the Cubans in the 1960s and again in the 1980s, and then the Vietnamese after that country was unified in the early 1970s. A new wave may be expected, if it has not already begun, from Hong

Kong when that territory becomes part of the People's Republic of China in a few years.

Unlike the earlier immigrants, a large number of whom became supporters of liberal domestic movements, the more recent arrivals—especially those from Cuba, Vietnam, and Eastern Europe—are either apolitical or extremely conservative and often intensely hostile to liberal social change. Their support has gone largely to the right side of the political spectrum. The economic immigrants (legal and illegal) from Central America and Mexico are so fearful of being deported that it is highly unlikely to expect, at least in the short term, their active and critical participation in the national political process.

Given time for a generation or two to be born in the United States, the new immigrants might well duplicate the political paths taken by the older immigrant waves. However, in contrast with the times of heavy immigration in the nineteenth and early twentieth centuries, the U.S. economy is no longer youthful and growing exuberantly. If anything, signs point to prolonged stagnation and contraction in the years ahead. Though it is risky to speculate on the behavior of large groups of people in a constrained and crisis-dominated period, the presence of substantial, conservatively inclined immigrant populations seems likely to make it still more difficult to effect the political and economic measures that may be required to safeguard the democratic social fabric in the years ahead.

Another far-reaching structural change has affected deeply and adversely the vigor of public expression and the democratic process in the country. This is the changed living locale for millions of Americans—the massive moves, begun immediately after the war, from the city to the suburbs to the exurbs and, most recently, to the connurbations generously described as "new cities." This shift in the ecology of living space and its significance for public expression are discussed in Chapter 5.

One further factor, one which could be called the "historical-transitional," for it is already past, deserves mention. This is "the good times" factor that characterized the postwar period until the onset of the world economic slowdown in the mid-'70s. Not by a long shot did everyone in the United States enjoy prosperity in the preceding thirty years; but enough did to create a cloud of euphoria. A brief challenge to the character of the state of economic success flared in the sixties and subsided almost as rapidly as it emerged. Here, we merely note the impact of the short-lived "good times" interval on the quality and focus of cultural expression.

Who Gets What in Postwar America:
The Material Payoff

The growth of corporate influence and power alongside the decline of once-strong, democratic oppositional forces—independent farmers and organized labor—and the influx of successive conservative immigrant waves constitute at least part of the infrastructural framework within which the cultural-informational developments of the last fifty years have unfolded. It is within this framework that the corporate enclosure of public expression and cultural creativity has proceeded.

But before turning to this main theme, a brief excursion into the present state of national resource allocation is an indispensable prerequisite to the analysis. It is indispensable because it explains, at least in part, what ties together all of the seemingly disparate activities in the economic, political, and cultural spheres. For underneath the media images, the political campaigns, and the economic decision-making, there is a common denominator, a unifying principle that is disarmingly plain and simple despite the efforts that are made to make it seem complex and obscure.

Simply put, the main objective of the American corporate economy is to maximize profits in whatever are the given circumstances. This requires being in charge of the key levers of power. Who is in control determines the answer to the first question that faces any social order: who gets what? The ascendance of the corporation to the position of major resource allocator in American life is nicely illustrated in the ordinarily unexciting, but very instructive, national tax and income distribution statistics (see table 1).

Over a thirty year interval from 1952 to 1983, income taxes paid by corporations dwindled to an insignificant 6.6 percent of all federal revenues from 32.1 percent in 1952. Over the same period, taxes on individuals have increased substantially, and payroll taxes (one of the most unfair of all levies) have nearly quadrupled as a percentage of all federal revenues. It is from payroll taxes that the revenues to finance Social Security and Medicare, for example, come. The surpluses from these taxes that have piled up (and will accumulate still more in forthcoming years) in the Reagan era are mountainous. Yet these taxes impose much heavier burdens on low-income earners than would taxes levied on a progressive, individual-income and corporate-income scale.

The trend toward tax inequality—unfair sharing of the costs of social existence—has accelerated in recent years. A Congressional Budget Office study reported that the "poorest one-tenth of Americans will

Table 1 The Shrinking Corporate Tax Burden (Major tax sources of Federal revenues and their share of the total for fiscal years)

TAXES	1952	1960	1970	1980	1981	1982	1983
Individual Income	42.2%	44.0%	46.9%	47.2%	47.7%	48.3%	47.2%
Corporation Income	**32.1**	**23.2**	**17.0**	**12.5**	**10.2**	**8.0**	**6.6**
Social insurance*	9.8	15.9	23.0	30.5	30.5	32.6	35.5
Excise	13.4	12.6	8.1	4.7	6.8	5.9	6.4
Estate and Gift	1.2	1.7	1.9	1.2	1.1	1.3	0.9
Other	1.4	2.5	3.0	3.9	3.7	4.0	3.5

Source: New York Times, March 20, 1987, with data from the U.S. Office of Management and Budget.

Note: Totals may not equal 100 percent due to rounding.

*Includes Social Security, Medicare, Unemployment, Railroad Retirement, and Federal Employee Retirement taxes.

pay 20 percent more of their earnings in Federal taxes in 1988 than they did in 1987 and the richest will pay almost 20 percent less."[22] The effect of this shifting of the tax burden from those who can afford to pay to those who cannot is one way to redistribute income. By the end of 1988, the Budget Office study concluded: "80 percent of families will have seen their income decline since 1977 when adjusted for inflation. . . . But the richest 10 percent will see an average increase of 16 percent, the top 5 percent will average a 23 percent rise and the richest 1 percent will see their income grow by 50 percent."[23]

This "invisible" income redistribution is the contribution of the postwar national administrations. It is also an indirect and generally unpublicized testimonial to the successful informational efforts and energies expended by the corporate sector and its media champions. How to account in an age of intensive publicity for such reticence about such a remarkable public relations achievement—the transfer of wealth from the poor to the rich without a sign of public indignation? Actually, this "achievement" may be regarded as one of the tangible outcomes of the corporate envelopment of public expression.

A precondition for this "achievement" has been the growth of the information-cultural industries where the messages and images that influence public consciousness are produced. It is the national consumption of this outflow that largely conditions the popular sense of (un)reality. It is to an account of the growth of these message-making industries that we now turn.

| 2 |

The Corporation and
the Production of Culture

The industries that serve as the sites for the creation, packaging, transmission, and placement of cultural messages—corporate ones especially—have grown greatly as their importance and centrality to the corporate economy increases. Many of the largest corporations, whatever their main activity, now possess their own communication facilities for message-making and transmission to local or national audiences. Nevertheless, the industries whose main function is the production of messages and imagery—those that can be seen as cultural industries in their own right—continue to be the main centers of symbolic production. A United Nations Scientific and Cultural Organization (UNESCO) study of these industries defined them in this way:

> Generally speaking, a cultural industry is held to exist when cultural goods and services are produced, reproduced, stored or distributed on industrial and commercial lines, that is to say on a large scale and in accordance with a strategy based on economic considerations rather than any concerns for cultural development.[1]

Included in the cultural industries are publishing, the press, film, radio, television, photography, recording, advertising, sports, and, most recently, the many components that now make up the information industry (data-base creation, production of software for computers, and various forms of salable information).

There is a "second tier" in the category of cultural industries. These activities also provide symbolic goods and services. The services, however, are displayed in relatively permanent installations, instead of being produced serially. Using this measure, museums, art galleries, amusement parks (Disneyland, Sea World—there are more than 600 theme and amusement parks in America), shopping malls, and corporate "public spaces" also function as culture industries.

It is not arbitrary to single out these activities and designate them as cultural industries. It can be maintained with justification that *all* economic activity produces symbolic as well as material goods. In fact, the two are generally inseparable. An automobile, in addition to being a vehicle of transport, is also a striking assemblage of symbols and provides a rich symbolic menu to its owner or aspiring purchaser. A pair of shoes is often much more than foot coverage and protection.

Actually, a community's economic life cannot be separated from its symbolic content. Together they represent the totality of a culture. Still, it is observable in the development of capitalism from its feudal origins that specific categories of symbolic goods and services have been withdrawn from their place in community and individual existence. They have been organized much like other branches of industrial activity, subject to the same rules of production and exchange.

Speech, dance, drama (ritual), music, and the visual and plastic arts have been vital, indeed necessary, features of human experience from earliest times. What distinguishes their situation in the industrial-capitalist era, and especially in its most recent development, are the relentless and successful efforts to separate these elemental expressions of human creativity from their group and community origins for the purpose of *selling them* to those who can pay for them.

In recent centuries, most markedly in the twentieth, cultural creation has been transformed into discrete, specialized forms, commercially produced and marketed. The common characteristics of cultural products today are the utilization of paid labor, the private appropriation of labor's creative product, and its sale for a profit. Jeremy Seabrook has written extensively on the *general process* of commercial production and acknowledges that there is greater efficiency. Productivity is higher and, consequently, the availability of goods is greater. But there is a cost, he notes, a very high cost! "The price paid by working people for the 'successes' of capitalism has been in terms of the breakdown of human associations, the loss of solidarity, indifference between people, violence, loneliness . . . and a sense of loss of function and purpose."[2] Describing the same process as it affects a modern cultural product—film—is this appraisal:

> . . . the objective character of film is its existence as a comodity. That it
> is made by wage labor, and that its purpose is exchange value, united it
> with virtually everything else in capitalism. . . . The producer of film is
> not, in reality, the person whose name flashes on the screen. That
> person is the surrogate who carries out the generalized logic of the
> institutional order in which the film industry exists. The ultimate pro-
> ducer of the commodity is the set of property relations that are specific
> to a historical epoch.[3]

The cultural goods and services of modern American cultural industries, therefore, are not outputs of ahistorical, universalistic creative
genius and talent. However much they may be appreciated, imitated,
or adopted elsewhere, they remain the specific cultural forms of a
particular set of institutional arrangements.

Market control of creativity and symbolic production has developed unevenly since the beginning of capitalism, some creative
fields possessing special features or offering greater resistance to
their commercial appropriation than others. The amount of money
(capital) required to enter a specific cultural industry has worked
either as a constraint—if the amount is considerable—or as an
encouragement—if the investment was minimal. Still, by the close of
the twentieth century, in highly developed market economies at
least, most symbolic production and human creativity have been
captured by and subjected to market relations. Private ownership of
the cultural means of production and the sale of the outputs for
profit have been the customary characteristics. The exceptions—
publicly supported libraries, museums, music—are few, and they are
rapidly disappearing. The last fifty years have seen an acceleration
in the decline of nonmarket-controlled creative work and symbolic
output. At the same time, there has been a huge growth in its
commercial production.

Parallel with the private appropriation of symbolic activity has
been the rationalization of its production. This includes the development of more efficient techniques and the invention of means to
expand the market output to a global scale. The production of goods
and services in the cultural sphere has indeed been industrialized. It is
in this respect that the term "cultural industries" assumes its meaning.

The expanded production and distribution capabilities have increased immeasurably the profitability of cultural production, though
this is generally left unremarked. Attention is directed instead to the
undeniable impressiveness of the new technologies of message-making
and transmission and their alleged potential for human enrichment.

For example, it is beyond question that cable television has the capability to offer substantially enlarged program diversity. But this is still to be demonstrated. There is no ambiguity, however, about the profitability of the new technology. The cable industry's revenues have jumped to above $16 billion in 1987, up from $1 billion in 1976.[4]

Another feature (mostly ignored) of the modern cultural industries is their deeply structured and pervasive ideological character. The heavy public consumption of cultural products and services and the contexts in which most of them are provided represent a daily, if not hourly, diet of systemic values, spooned out to whichever public happens to be engaged. "The typical film from which investors anticipate a profit," writes film analyst Thomas Guback, "may be art or non-art, but it is always a commodity."[5] The same can be said for Broadway musical comedies, best-selling novels, and top-of-the-chart records. They are commodities and ideological products, embodying the rules and values of the market system that produced them. Multi-million-dollar investments in film, theater, or publishing can be relied upon to contain systemic thinking. In the late twentieth century, those few spaces that have escaped incorporation into the market are being subjected to continuous pressure and, often, frontal attack.

Trends In the Cultural Industries: The New Technologies

Over the course of the last one hundred years, a succession of inventions and technological innovations have produced the means by which certain kinds of cultural production could be expanded enormously. The instantaneous and universal dissemination of cultural outputs is also now technically feasible—though in some instances political factors may operate as limiting conditions.

The improved efficiency of the printing press and the invention of radio, television, cable, fiber optics, the communication satellite, and the computer have transformed communication. Yet the revolutionized instrumentation and the communication process itself remain, for the most part (certainly in the United States), firmly anchored in market relations. Occasionally, there have been some hybrid arrangements, but overall, a market context for the new communication technologies continues to prevail.

This being the case, the great increase in penetrability made possible by the new technologies has created a marketing ideological atmosphere that smothers the senses domestically and is rapidly doing the

same globally. The cultural industries have become an integral component of the market economy, and their sales messages, in a remarkable variety of ways, fill public, private, and personal space.

The communication satellite makes message penetrability global.
Recent Olympic Games were viewed, it is claimed, by a billion specta-
tors. This is ideological and marketing diffusion beyond the wildest
dreams of early twentieth-century prophets of salesmanship—who,
by the way, were not shy in their goals and expectations. The cultural
industries are booming as their outputs reach domestic audiences of
tots to nonagenarians and are exported as well to worldwide markets.
The *Wall Street Journal* reports that "The media-blitzed child of the
80's is proving highly brand-conscious. . . . The interest in labels
starts early." Dale Wallenius, publisher of the *Marketing to Kids
Report,* says, "Even two-year-olds are concerned about their brand of
clothes, and by the age of six are full-out consumers."[6] And, of
course, the sales message appears in a variety of ways in addition to
standard advertising. This is perhaps the cultural industries' greatest
achievement.

The great upsurge in the cultural industries cannot be explained
exclusively, however, on the basis of improved technical capabilities.
Credit also must be given to social developments that the market
economy itself has promoted. As the output of all material goods and
services steadily rises, a wide array of supportive activities comes into
existence to facilitate their distribution and consumption and even the
public awareness of their existence. Advertising, installment credit,
personal finance, banking, insurance, retailing, and transport follow
closely the expansion of the manufacturing system. In nation after
nation, employees in the new fields eventually outnumber workers
producing goods. The workers who fill these new occupations now
constitute the bulk of the U.S. work force. They have more school-
ing. They are urban- and suburban-domiciled. They have more time
away from the work site. Their families are increasingly, of necessity
in many cases, composed of two wage earners.

These conditions combine to bestow an ever-greater importance to
the images and messages of the cultural industries. The social "glue,"
such as it is, of the advanced market economy is provided by a steady
diet of news, sports, film, TV comedy and drama, entertainment
"parks," tourist excursions, and footage of distant wars and conflicts.
The fragmentation and privatization of living arrangements, experience, personal interactions, and total being are alleviated or con-
cealed by "spectaculars" produced by the cultural industries: "Su-

perbowls"; best-sellers; celebrity talk shows; blockbuster movies; and a dizzying cycle of new foods, styles, fashions, and prescriptions for eating, fasting, managing, and succeeding.

In creating and satisfying the huge national appetite for cultural product, the industries engaged in its manufacture exhibit the same economic trends as did the industries in the preceding industrial era. In that period, the size of the enterprise expanded to take advantage of economies of scale in production, as well as to have on hand the resources needed to exploit opportunities (markets) as they arose, nationally and eventually internationally. The pattern is no different in the cultural industries in the 1980s. A prediction made in the mid-1980s that by 1995 almost 90 percent of all communication facilities (including newspapers, broadcast outlets, cable systems, telephone lines, relays, and satellites) would be in the hands of fifteen companies is close to realization well before that date. Ben Bagdikian, veteran journalist and former dean of the University of California's (Berkeley) Graduate School of Journalism, reported in 1987 how much "progress" to that end had been made:

> In 1982, when I completed research for my book, *The Media Monopoly,* 50 corporations controlled half or more of the media business. By December 1986, when I finished a revision for the second edition, the 50 had shrunk to 29. The last time I counted, it was down to 26.[7]

In the first edition of *The Media Monopoly* (1983), Bagdikian declared that "The fifty men and women [sic] who head these corporations would fit in a large room."[8] In 1987, a much smaller room would have been more than adequate.

These super-aggregations of resources in the cultural-informational sphere are the outcome of internal growth, from spectacular profits (especially in the television, cable, and film branches), and from never-ending connsolidations in corporate media and informational activities. The trend is observable in all the industries. *Business Week,* for example, describes Madison Avenue "looking like merger street . . . advertising agencies are gobbling each other up with the ardor they once reserved for bellowing 'new and improved.' "[9]

Mergers in the advertising business are typical of the other cultural industries. They derive from the changing character of the world economy and the growing share of the world market dominated by transnational corporations in general. "Multinationals now account for 20 percent of all advertising and their percentage is growing," notes the president of Young and Rubicam, one of the world's top ad agencies. "You have to be able to serve your client everywhere," he adds.[10]

The one exception—and a qualified one at that—to the transnationalization of the cultural industries is the press. For newspapers especially, it is the national and, even more, the local/regional market that is determining. Here, the objective is exclusivity. Local monopoly is the key to maximum advertising revenues. This explains why "of the 1700 daily papers [in the United States], 98 percent are local monopolies and fewer than 15 corporations control most of the country's daily circulation."[11]

Efforts to start new, competing papers have all but disappeared. And no wonder! The costs are prohibitive. One instance in recent years of a sustained attempt to launch a national newspaper is the *USA Today* undertaking. Since 1982, when *USA Today* first appeared, its operating losses in five years neared half a billion dollars. This figure does not include an additional $208 million for capital costs and the expense of employees borrowed from other papers in the Gannett Company chain, a chain now numbering over 90 newspapers.[12] Who could afford such outlays, other than a billion-dollar media conglomerate with a chairman of the board obsessed with controlling a national organ of opinion? And what does this tell us about the open marketplace for ideas in the 1980s as well as the insistence on First Amendment rights for billion-dollar corporate "individuals"?

Television, a medium with totally different physical characteristics, requires still more gargantuan capital requirements for entry. An independent television station in Los Angeles was sold in 1985 for $510 million. ABC's New York City affiliate with a potential audience in the millions has an estimated price tag of $800 million.

A wave of mergers in the 1980s placed some of the cultural industries at the financial as well as the informational center of the transnational corporate economy. The American Broadcasting company was acquired by Capital Cities, a deal that at the time was the largest merger outside the oil industry in U.S. history. It has since been surpassed. Another already huge conglomerate, Metromedia, itself bought out, sold seven key television stations to Rupert Murdoch and a partner for $2 billion. Murdoch already owned 20th Century-Fox and with the new acquisitions launched a fourth national television network. CBS, regarded by some as the media establishment, has been fighting off one takeover bid after another.

The publishing industry, a less flamboyant branch of the cultural industries, is no less caught up in the merger mania and cross-media combinations. Gulf and Western, already the owner of Paramount Studios and Simon and Schuster, acquired Prentice Hall, the largest textbook publisher in the United States. With these acquisitions, Gulf and Western, among its other activities, is now the largest "publishing house" in the world. The Newhouse publishing chain, owner of innumerable medium-size city newspapers, bought *The New Yorker,* adding it to other publishing holdings that include Random House, Alfred A. Knopf, Pantheon, Villard, Times Books, and Vintage Books.

What it means to function as a cultural industry in publishing—historically a small-scale commercial activity and only recently transformed by industrial conglomeration—is suggested in the evolution of the author-publisher relationship in textbook production. "When I first came into the field," explained David P. Amerman, vice president and director of the college division of Prentice Hall, in 1977, "the way you published a book was to find an academic with a reputation and hope he could write." Amerman observed that then "The book was essentially the author's." Ten years later, "We're exercising our muscle, and telling the author the best way to do it, a lot more than we used to." The *Chronicle of Higher Education,* in which this interview appeared, noted that "While the wholly 'managed' book is still a rarity in publishing, the 'author-assisted' book is a growing phenomenon." Mr. Amerman footnotes this: "We want control over the vocabulary."[13]

But it is not only the author's "vocabulary" that is monitored and managed. The writer's personality as well is now being appropriated and reworked for the marketing effort. The director of publicity for Macmillan, one of the oldest and most prestigious publishing firms, claims that it is not enough for an author to write a book. "Now you also have to sell it."[14] To prepare for this new task, writers are taking lessons on how to talk well to sell well on TV and radio. As talk shows have become a critical factor in the mass marketing of books, the author now has to sell self as well as book.

Contributing still more pressure for commercialization of the book is the growth of a few nationwide book chains—B. Dalton, Walden Books, Barnes & Noble, Crown, and Kroch's & Brentano's, etc. Though their denial of having any influence on the content of what is being published is unanimous, these big retail chains by their choice and promotions largely determine which books will become the big sellers. Their choices, in turn, are finely tuned to selecting works that have the greatest sales potential. While this criterion does not absolutely preclude material that is unfamiliar, socially critical, or seriously antiestablishment, it limits severely the likelihood of its publication—or at least publication by the main commercial houses.

The "Shyness" of the Cultural Industries

In contrast with their willingness to examine *individual* behavior in microscopic detail, the cultural industries—the mass media in particular—are remarkably reticent to examine their own activities. Commentary on the extensive merger movement in the media is illustrative. It receives substantial but essentially unilluminating coverage. Mostly, it is portrayed as entrepreneurial jousting.

Just as round-the-clock "soaps" and happy-talk news shows trivialize life's dilemmas and reduce them to personal strengths and weaknesses, structural changes in the informational system are presented generally in terms of an individual's character and energy. Accordingly, one is asked to consider whether Ted Turner is morally fit to run CBS. Will he endanger that network's status as—what founder and former chairman of the board William Paley called—a public trust? Will S. I. Newhouse quash *The New Yorker*'s vaunted editorial independence? Will Rupert Murdoch's down-market *New York Post* be taken away from him as a consequence of Senator Kennedy's vendetta against Murdoch's Boston newspaper holding? (It was.)

While the public is asked to reflect on these sideline and basically irrelevant issues, the cultural industries are responding boldly to the uncertainties and opportunities of highly fluid world and national markets. Far from merely reacting, the big media-cultural combines have become major initiators in the rapidly emerging transnational information system. Taking advantage of the pro-profit, anti-union, social accountability-be-damned climate of the Reagan years, media owners and other resource holders are maneuvering freely in the cultural and informational fields. They are concentrating their holdings to better exploit the domestic market and to penetrate the international market with information goods and services, messages and images. The smell of profits and the lure of global information dominance pervade the media-merger arena.

And so it goes, in film, cable television, network TV, radio, and throughout the cultural industries. In film, for example, "every big studio is now a conglomerate or has been purchased by a conglomerate," writes a Hollywood reporter. "For 1988," he notes, "the buzzword in Hollywood is vertical integration. The major studios—

and even some of the minor ones—intend to make and distribute movies, manufacture and sell video cassettes six months later, then syndicate their films to their own television stations, by-passing the networks, and, in the case of Disney, play them on a studio-owned pay-cable channel."[15] The four biggest "studios" are now subordinated to huge conglomerates, which, in turn, own sports teams, movie theater chains, television networks, cable systems, and much else. The president of the Writers Guild of America, for example, describing negotiations for a contract between writers and movie and television producers, noted: "We weren't negotiating with Paramount, but with Coca-Cola."[16]

The recent absorption of movie theaters by the big film companies violates a Supreme Court ruling of the late 1940s that forbade such ownership.[17] Today, indifferent to that forty-year-old injunction, a few studios hold about the same proportion of theaters that was ruled illegal a generation or more ago.[18] One immediate, visible effect of this development has been the practical elimination of art theaters that used to show foreign and domestic films that were not likely to be smash commercial hits. The larger consideration, not unrelated to the former, is that commercial criteria now totally dominate the industry. "The movies have always been an uneasy blend of art and commerce," observes one Hollywood commentator, "but today, commerce is the clear winner."[19]

The late screenwriter and film critic, Lester Cole, experienced the hard commercial side of the film industry firsthand fifty years ago. Running as a central thread throughout his account of the early Hollywood years is the aggressive, anti-union tactics of the egomaniacal moguls of that era. Cole himself was never forgiven for his persistent efforts to organize the film work force. Indeed, it was his militancy on behalf of film workers that put him in jail in the great Hollywood witch-hunt and purge of the 1940s.[20]

The degree of concentration already reached in the cable TV industry, with its multitudinous channels which were supposed to exorcise monopoly control, is striking. "The top four operators now control one-third of cable subscribers," and one company alone, Tele-Communications, has about 18.5 percent of the nation's total subscribers. Additionally, the nation's second-largest cable company, American Television and Communication Corporation, is owned by Time, Inc., the giant magazine conglomerate.[21] At the same time, Geraldine Fabricant reports in the *New York Times* that "cable operators which own the wires and boxes, or hardware, are also gobbling up substantial portions of the software—the shows, movies and sporting events that the cable carries."[22] Meanwhile, the monthly cable connection charges of more than forty-five million subscribers (in 1988) constitute an endless golden flow of revenues to a few super-corporations—who view any effort to make them take into account the social needs of the locales in which they operate as a violation of *their* First Amendment rights.

Radio is described and evaluated by the trade magazine *Radio & Records* as "little more than electronic real estate, and spectrum space is probably the most valuable asset in the United States."[23]

What is the significance of this awesome concentration of private cultural power? For one thing, it means that only the richest groups, nationally and internationally, can afford to own media-informational companies. What follows from this is that these holdings are the means for transmitting the thinking and the perspectives of the dominant, though tiniest, stratum of the propertied class, not only in news but also in entertainment and general cultural product.

At the beginning of the 1980s, well before some of the greatest media consolidations were effected, the UNESCO study already cited reflected on the concentration of control "and the subordination of artists to market forces." It speculated further:

> It is open to question, in order to obtain an accurate portrayal of the system of forces at work in the cultural industries, the assumed symmetry of classical communication theories should not be replaced by a firmly asymmetrical view, *reflecting the predominant influence of the industrial producer of the messages (or the interests backing him), who in the end dictates the choice of channel, the content and even the consumer's taste, in the interests of economic or ideological control.*[24]

It is precisely this view that is rejected by current communication and media theorists.

In fact, the presence of giantism and concentrated control in the media and allied cultural fields, though hardly a secret, now seems perfectly reasonable to most Americans—and certainly no cause for anxiety. The extent to which the public has been programmed to accept these conditions in the media, and in the economy overall, is remarkable. Especially so when it is remembered that throughout the nineteenth and the first half of the twentieth centuries, powerful antimonopoly social movements flourished in the country. As recently as fifty years ago, an American president, Franklin D. Roosevelt, could touch a responsive populist chord in the country by denouncing the "moneychangers in the temple" and the "economic royalists." In the early years of the century, Theodore Roosevelt attacked "the malefactors of great wealth."[25]

In contrast, in the 1980s, major industrial companies, and the press as well, boast about and insist upon the virtue of their enormous assets. The Hearst Corporation, for example (in an earlier time synonymous with the abuse of press power), now announces in public advertisements:

> The Hearst Centennial. 100 Years of Making Communication History. Hearst is more than 135 businesses, including magazines, broadcasting, newspapers, books, business publishing and cable communications.[26]

Similarly, the Gannett Corporation brazenly assures the public time and again that its ownership of more than 90 newspapers and a clutch of television and radio stations across the country is a guarantor of diversity and pluralism.[27]

The Los Angeles Times Mirror Company, which includes among its holdings, the *Los Angeles Times,* the *Denver Post,* the *Baltimore Sun,* and the *Hartford Courant,* along with other magazines, newspapers, cable and broadcast interests, recently released a plan whereby its chief owners (the Chandler family) and a few other big shareholders could permanently retain control of the company. A spokesperson for the company explained that the maintenance of this control "promote(s) continued independence and integrity of our media operations for the benefit of our shareholders and for the public served by our various media interests."[28] It is not difficult to see that the benefits to the major shareholders, including the Chandler family, will be promoted. It is less easy to see what the public gains from an arrangement that vests control in perpetuity to a tiny group of wealthy stockholders. The notion that "independence and integrity" is guaranteed by such ownership is one of the myths that the media, the press in particular, have cultivated successfully for a very long time.

Rupert Murdoch, another media mogul with international holdings, was exercised because he was ordered to comply with a mild Federal Communications Commission ruling limiting cross-media holdings, i.e., ownership of a TV station and a newspaper by the same interests in one locale. What was seen not so long ago as an elementary and far from sweeping step to assure diversity in a city or region is in the late 1980s treated by arrogant media owners and their political sycophants as arbitrary intervention of the state and as a violation of their First Amendment rights. In this particular case, Murdoch was compelled to sell his New York City newspaper, the *New York Post.*[29]

The two senators from the state of New York argued that this ruling constituted a hardship on the city because jobs would be lost if the *Post* could not be sold and was forced to liquidate. This was a totally unrealistic scenario. The paper was sold. The brand of thinking by Murdoch's defenders discounted media and informational monopoly as long as it offered employment. This is of a piece with the rationale for defense/military expenditures.

Countervailing Pressure on the Cultural Industries?

Despite the pyramiding of assets and combinations of media interests in recent decades, the concentrated cultural industries are not the exclusive players in the message-making business. In many fields (publishing, recording, and, to a much lesser extent, in film and television), numerous small producers do manage to carry on and from time to time produce nationally acclaimed material. This is not, however, a contradiction or an offset to power and in no way diminishes the general dominance of the big players.

Actually, some small-scale production is one means of "managing creativity."[30] It has evolved and been refined to rationalize the handling of a stubbornly recalcitrant yet indispensable resource used in the cultural industries: human creativity. In allowing small-scale and relatively independent activity to continue to exist in cultural work, the big cultural firms insure a constant supply of talent and creativity that otherwise might be ignored or even suffocated in their own bureaucratized, symbol-making factories. The "independents" are continually tapped to replenish exhausted creative energies in the cultural conglomerates. The trick for the latter is to keep the creative juices flowing—but inside channels that reliably lead back to the main conduits.

This objective is achieved primarily by insuring that the cultural production process, monopoly-size or small-scale independent, remains securely anchored in market relations. Privatized message and symbol production binds the producers, large and small, in interdependent relationships in which small players are "more interdependent"—less independent—than the big actors. By the same means, the *content* of the cultural product is no less subject to the market imperative—profitability—wherever it originates.

The ideological component, if marginally more open in independent, smaller-scale productions, overall remains pliable to the corporate voice. Independent producers, as well as executives in the big cultural enterprises, may have *personal* standards and preferences for honest, well-produced subject matter. But whatever the individual inclination, the determining factor in the large majority of decisions about what products and services are made *must be* commercial profitability.

Consider the experience of Pare Lorenz, the director of some of the most powerful social documentaries of the 1930s: *The Plow That Broke the Plains, The River, The Fight for Life.* Lorenz was "saluted" by the Academy of Motion Picture Arts and Sciences in 1981. Yet he made his last film, *The Nuremberg Trials,* in 1946. Since then he has been unable to secure financing for his projects. A documentary attempted in 1948 about the atomic test on the Bikini atoll could not be continued. Lorenz noted simply: "We couldn't raise two dollars and a half."[31] Lorenz's experience is by no means exceptional. New York City and Los Angeles are filled with independent producers of film and video desperately trying to raise insignificant amounts of money to continue or to begin projects.

If a creative project, no matter what its inherent quality, cannot be viewed as a potential money-maker, salable in a large enough market, its production is problematic at best. This in no way means that all projects that are approved, will, in fact, be money-makers. In a society that fosters consumption, taste and fashion must change rapidly and unceasingly. The larger the cultural enterprise, the greater its resources to finance "mistakes." At the same time, there is also the likelihood of more expensive misjudgments. The cultural industries, no different than the rest of American industry, try to minimize risk. But risk and instability are inherent in capitalist enterprise in general.

To the extent then that the creative process has been absorbed by industries producing for the market, the commercial imperative prevails. General awareness that profitability is the ultimate determinant of cultural production becomes internalized in the creative mindset. Scriptwriters, authors, videomakers, and film directors shape their efforts, consciously or not, with rare exceptions to the deep-structured demands of salability and prospective return.

Even those who may appear to be the last holdouts of individual creativity, the studio artists working alone, find no escape from the market imperative, though the pressure may be brought to bear in less explicit ways. The gallery system, private collectors, art speculators, and the process of museum acquisition constitute a special but in no way fundamentally different commercial framework than television networks that commission shows from TV production companies.

As the cultural industries increasingly occupy pivotal positions of social, political, and even economic power in the latest period of capitalist development, their symbolic outputs, however entertaining, diverting, esthetic, or informative, are essentially elements of corporate expression. Corporate speech, therefore, has become an integral part of cultural production in general. Most imagery and messages, products and services are now corporately fashioned from their origin to their manufacture and dissemination. Consider, for example, the making and distribution of the successful 1988 movie, *Who Framed Roger Rabbit:*

> Walt Disney Co. spent $45 million to make Spielberg's *Who Framed Roger Rabbit* and has committed an additional $10 million to promote it. Coke and McDonald's Corp. will spend an estimated $22 million on ad and promotional campaigns linked to the movie. They hope the hit movie's magic will rub off on diet Coke and Big Mac. Disney, in turn, figures that Roger Rabbit's ubiquity, courtesy of Coke and McDonald's, translates into some $20 million in extra ad exposure for the movie.

Additionally, "some 30 licensees will market toys, jackets and jewelry based on *Roger Rabbit.*"[32]

The corporate "voice" now constitutes the national symbolic environment. For this reason, as one artist sees it, "it becomes more and more difficult to maintain the difference between individual and corporate speech. Differences between forms of address become harder to sustain, or even perceive."[33]

It is not so much that one or another corporate giant utilizes the cultural industries to make its preferences known to the public. This, of course, is a continuing and pervasive feature of the domestic cultural landscape. Far more significant is the organic process by which the corporate "voice" is generalized across the entire range of cultural expression. Writing of another place and another time, Henry Glassie's commentary is especially appropriate here:

> If people are stripped of the ability to manipulate truth, to make their own things and their own history, they may continue to act properly, but they lose the capacity to think for themselves about their own rightness. They stagnate or surrender. If truth is located beyond the mind's grasp, if it is something that exists but cannot be touched, then culture cannot be advanced or defended. Made consumers, spectators, restrained from

voluntary action, people become slaves, willing or not, happy or not, of powers that want their bodies. Those who steal from people their right to make artifacts (in order to sell junk to them) and those who steal their right to make their own history (in order to destroy their will to cultural resistance)—these can be condemned, for they steal from people the right to know what they know, the right to become human.[34]

It is this systematic envelopment of human consciousness by corporate speech in America in the 1980s that we discuss next.

| 3 |

The Corporation and the Law

The cultural industries have been spectacular growth centers in post-World War II America. Huge corporate conglomerates of message and image production have emerged. At the same time, the influence of corporate expression has extended well beyond the specific sites of film, TV, radio, the press, and publishing. The entire arena of national life is now the locale of corporate perspectives, expressed in an enormous variety of outlets and channels, recreational and otherwise. Once the corporate business system discovered that communication and culture were profitable as well as politically expedient, it was only a matter of time—a very short time—before the scope of corporate expression, up to the 1970s severely limited by law, was broadened.

In 1942, the Supreme Court ruled in a unanimous, three-page decision[1] that commercial speech was *not* entitled to the protection of the First Amendment. This opinion was delivered, as political commentator Robert Sherrill tellingly points out, when the Court had two of the most steadfast defenders of free speech in its long history, Justice Hugo Black and Justice William Douglas.[2] Forty-five years later, a barrage of advertising, along with corporate media pronouncements on almost every facet of political, cultural, and economic life, is transmitted and afforded some constitutional protection.

The change in the status of corporate commercial and political speech over a few decades is nothing less than extraordinary. In a work devoted to the subject, it is described as "a remarkable ideological inversion."[3] How and why did this "inversion" come about, and why did the judicial system wait so long to grant corporations First Amendment privileges? It is indeed "peculiar," as legal scholar Mark Tushnet observed, "that the Court came so late to the recognition that the governing metaphors of free speech theory and of life in capitalist society supported constitutional protection of corporate speech."[4] It *is* peculiar because the courts historically have provided reliable support for the private enterprise system. This is confirmed in a cursory review of American law.[5]

At each stage in the development of the American economy, from the earliest days of the republic, Court rulings either protected or reinforced what at the time constituted the basic form of private property.[6] Before the Civil War, property in the United States was largely small-scale and land-based. Great industrial growth and increasing concentration of capital were marked features of the post-Civil War period. The private corporation became the dominant form of enterprise with its capacity to accumulate and concentrate capital. The judicial system responded to these developments.

In 1886, the Supreme Court in a landmark ruling voted unanimously that corporations were "persons" and consequently were entitled to the protection of the equal protection clause of the Fourteenth Amendment.[7] This "fiction" enabled corporations to take advantage of the "due process" clause of the Fourteenth Amendment and to shield themselves from regulatory action that might be proposed on behalf of the community or the work force. The corporation as a person could not be deprived of its property or managerial authority without "due process." In effect, and in historical reality, corporations could not be made socially accountable except under the most limited and circumscribed conditions. Indeed, this made accountability almost nonexistent. More specifically, with this ruling, writes Sherrill, "the inequality between white and black that the 14th Amendment was supposed to overcome has instead been transformed into perhaps an even greater inequality between the corporate person and the natural person."[8] Thus, historian Howard Zinn notes that although the Fourteenth Amendment "had been passed to protect Negro rights. . . . Of the Fourteenth Amendment cases brought before the Supreme Court between 1890 and 1910, nineteen dealt with the Negro, 288 dealt with corporations."[9]

With the decision of 1886 then, the era of "economic due process" was launched. In what was to be a long-lasting period, corporate property was protected against those social claims that would have required state intervention. The economic-due-process era prevailed until the outbreak of the profound economic crisis of the 1930s. Then the traumatic collapse of the American economic machine compelled the government to take actions, mandated by New Deal legislation, that frequently interfered with what had become corporate prerogatives over property. For a brief time, the due-process clause—limiting government intervention in economic life—lost some of its sacrosanct quality. Measures of social control were acceptable because capitalism itself was on the defensive and hardly capable of asserting its immunity to public accountability.

The outbreak of the Second World War restored vitality to the American economy—unlike its impact elsewhere. Corporate business, temporarily weakened in the prewar decade, experienced formidable expansion. Additionally, fed on superprofits from the war and luxuriating in the physical destruction of overseas competition, the corporate sector helped bring into being and benefitted further from the first consumer society. Tax-privileged home mortgages, automobile installment credit, and relatively full employment, as well as exports to war-damaged Europe and elsewhere, were the basis for this "new" society.

A number of extraordinary, new communication technologies, many derived from wartime applications, were introduced into the civilian economy. Television came into wide use in the late 1940s. It was supplemented in a few years with cable and satellite transmission. In the 1960s, computers and computer networks, available to the military for years, became part of the national, civilian information infrastructure as well. The introduction of these technologies had important consequences. They became the bases of new industries and greatly facilitated the growth of existing ones. Those fields which were closely associated with the management of property—banking, insurance, real estate—especially benefitted. The enormously enhanced capability of the new instrumentation to generate, transmit, store, and retrieve data and messages provided the indispensable infrastructure of the large corporations, especially of those that had become active in the international market.

Also, mainly as a result of these new informational means, the social opposition movements that emerged in this period were able to reach hitherto unavailable audiences. Civil-rights activists, environmentalists, anti-Vietnam War protestors, women's and consumer movements, and later the general peace movement have been beneficiaries, in varying degree, of the newer modes of message creation and transmission. At the same time, misrepresentation and distortion were facilitated.

What is of special relevance here, however, is that these several social movements and their public expression collided with the power structure, corporate enterprise in particular. And so, strong as the corporate enterprise sector had grown in the immediate postwar period, the challenges to its legitimacy and privileged position multiplied. These contradictory developments combined to produce a new configuration of property, power, and legitimation. American private industrial power now coexists with a no less influential private informational sector which has the capacity either to greatly strengthen or to deeply damage the entire corporate sector.

And so, just as industry replaced agriculture as the dominant economic activity in the late nineteenth century, information-producing and -using industries have begun to gain primacy in the waning years of the twentieth. Information flows are vital to the global operations of the most powerful transnational companies. The free flow of business information has become the nonnegotiable objective of U.S. international diplomacy—which, not surprisingly, presents its case as a universal, humanistic good, not as a corporate necessity.

Domestically and internationally, proprietary control of information has assumed strategic importance. Data bases and computer software constitute new forms of intellectual property. The International Chamber of Commerce, more aware than most of these developments, solicits governments "to make protection of intellectual property a matter of international discussion."[10]

Access to and influence over the means of communication, mostly the mass media, are more important than ever. Now enlisted in the frontline defense of corporate operations, the media serve as well in the strengthening of the system at large, domestically and internationally. "Should big corporations use their power to influence public opinion?" reads a quarter-page ad on the op-ed page of the *New York Times*. "You bet," says Herb Schmerz, at the time Mobil Oil's vice president for public affairs. "Corporations have as much right as anyone to plead their case before the public. If they don't speak out on crucial issues, the voice of business is in danger of being drowned out by the chorus of its critics."[11] Another "threatened voice" from the oil industry, the editor of Exxon's journal, *Exxon USA,* ruminates, ". . . if you can inject enough facts into the minds of people who direct public opinion, you can blunt criticism in advance."[12]

What does this add up to? The expanded protection offered corporate commercial and political speech, fashioned in a series of court decisions since the mid-1960s and the early 1970s (culminating in landmark rulings in 1978 and 1980), can be understood best as the latest stage in the historical, judicial accommodation to and promotion of property rights in the United States.

Information as property and the use and control of information to defend propety are distinctive characteristics of capitalism in the concluding years of the twentieth century. The capability of giant corporations to engage in information activities, either in pursuit of specific business objectives or in the promotion of general systemic interests, has become indispensable. Describing an "outpouring of corporate eloquence" since the 1970s, one writer found it "[a] . . . movement that has outgrown its earlier roots in the special interests of particular firms and become really classwide."[13] The Supreme Court's commercial and corporate speech decisions can be interpreted, in this context, as the adaptation of the law to the needs of an information-using corporate economy.

In coming to this conclusion, one qualification is necessary. There has been no linear, direct, one-to-one relationship between the needs of the corporate system overall and the specific decisions of the Supreme Court. In fact, contradictions and surprising reversals have marked the course of recent corporate-speech rulings. All the same, from the mid-1960s to the late 1970s, a number of decisions—taken cumulatively—overturned the Court's unequivocal 1942 ruling that commercial speech was *not* entitled to constitutional protection. The arguments for corporate-speech protection, and the parties that have made them, reveal some of the complexity and the paradoxes that characterize the sweeping legal shifts of recent years—which may not yet be concluded.

One unusual feature of the largely successful effort to confer legitimacy on corporate speech was the identity of the parties seeking the right to advertise in the 1960s and 1970s. Invariably, they were *not* the major transnational corporations. On the contrary, they were social groups whose activities and objectives were generally far from being profit-making or -seeking. They included consumers who wanted information on drug prices[14], clinics advertising abortion facilities to women[15], and those seeking to protect civil rights and to safeguard integrated housing.[16]

Another point that is noteworthy about these cases and Court rulings which granted limited constitutional rights to commercial messages was the *content* of the advertising. It was for social goals. This, apparently, was influential with the more liberal Court justices.

The problem of media access was already a major deterrent, and the initiatives taken by the issue-oriented groups, of necessity, compelled them to resort to commercial channels. Their numerical strength was small, their networks were minimal, their material resources scanty. Commercial advertising seemed one of the few means by which their social views could receive a hearing.

Yet, once the step was taken to constitutionally support, at least in part, commercial speech, a very different kind of "speaker" quickly made an appearance. Ithiel de Sola Pool commented on this later in his analysis of a 1976 drug-price case, *Virginia Board of Pharmacy v. Citizens Consumer Council.* "There could be no better way," he reflected, "for the advertising industry to make its case for the validity of freedom to advertise than in a suit [brought] by the consumer movement."[17]

In instances like this, which have occurred so often in the information-cultural sphere, the enticing though ultimately illusory prospect of social benefits accruing to the many served to ease the way for the commercial interests of the few. Without the pretext of serving the general interest, the privileged minority could never gain popular support. It has gone thus in radio, television, cable, and satellite transmission. Always the new technologies have been introduced with the promise of "cultural enrichment for all," "education for the disadvantaged," greater diversity and technology to integrate the most remote and deprived hamlet. The outcome over the last sixty years—with few exceptions—has been the preemption of the new means of communication for corporate, commercial advantage. Accordingly, the well-heeled "speakers" were not slow in making their appearance.

Once the first step of the bestowal of First Amendment rights to advertisers had been taken, successive steps came relatively quickly. In 1978, the Supreme Court issued a ruling to extend some First Amendment protection to corporate political speech in the *First National Bank of Boston v. Bellotti* decision[18] and refined the entire corporate speech doctrine in two additional rulings in 1980: *Consolidated Edison Co. of New York, Inc. v. Public Service Commission of New York*[19] and *Central Hudson Gas & Electric Corp. v. Public Service Commission of New York.*[20] In *Bellotti,* the Supreme Court overturned the Massachusetts Supreme Court and ruled that a corporation could make contributions or expenditures for the purpose of influencing state referenda, whether or not the issue being decided materially affected the company's property or business interests. In *Central Hudson Gas and Electric,* decided two years later, the Court amplified its rationale for the support of the corporate-speech doctrine. At the same time, it set down as well some stringent tests for determining when corporate speech could be regulated by the state. In effect, this elevated commercial speech to almost the same level as editorial speech—for that too under certain exceptional conditions can be suppressed by the state.

With the *Bellotti* decision, the right of a corporation to engage in the political process and, by extension, in cultural affairs in general was affirmed. It "was an occasion," one account observed, "for dancing not only in the streets but in the corporate boardrooms as well."[21] The thinking of the Court in this case is of exceptional interest because it set forth the essential doctrine while at the same time renewing some frayed myths. These now sustain a massive presence of the private corporation in most of the spaces of American life and culture. Above everything else, *Bellotti* reasserted and gave fresh vigor to the near-century-old, extraordinary ruling that made corporations into the equivalent of legal persons. Justice Powell, speaking for the majority of the Court, stated this flatly: "It has been settled for almost a century that corporations are persons within the meaning of the Fourteenth Amendment."[22]

In the 1980s, however, the corporation is a "person" with substantially expanded rights when compared to the far-from-deprived corporate "person" of one hundred years ago. The corporate "person" today is endowed with limited but still considerable First Amendment–protected rights of speech. It is legitimized to participate in the production, exchange, and dissemination of information. In short, in the contemporary computerized and transnationalized economic order, corporations, in addition to selling their goods and services in global markets, are allowed to express their views and perspectives on issues that affect people everywhere.

Almost defying comprehension, the significance of according speech rights to a corporate "person" passed practically unremarked by the Court's majority. In fact, the extent to which First Amendment speech rights were sidestepped was extraordinary. This was accomplished largely by focusing "The Court's opinion on the nature of the speech itself, rather than on the source of the speech."[23] This was in keeping with the commercial-speech doctrine that the Court had been developing over the preceding decade and a half. In general terms, it gave priority, if not preponderant weight, to the *rights of the recipient*—the receiver of the information and messages. This approach, whatever its intention, neatly redirected attention *away* from the message's source *to* the message's receiver.

The emphasis on receiver's rights, expressed in rulings preceding *Bellotti* as well,[24] rested heavily on the misuse of the views of Alexander Meiklejohn, who was a strong believer in democratic decision-making. Meiklejohn's ideas, write the chroniclers of corporate-speech doctrine, "are the theoretical foundations of the doctrines of 'listeners' rights, which in turn, is the foundation of both First Amendment protection of commercial speech and First Amendment protection of corporate speech addressed to political and public questions."[25]

But Meiklejohn, writing in the early post-World War II period, was concerned that the public should hear all views on an issue and that the arena of decision-making be as wide as possible. Democratic decisions in Meiklejohn's thinking would be arrived at in town-meeting-like settings, in which all citizens participated as equals. It was in a context then of rough equality in status and free exchange of ideas—*by individuals*—not "legal persons"—that Meiklejohn gave primacy to the rights of listeners. Meiklejohn's town meeting was not envisaged as a forum for corporate expression. As one commentator, not especially supportive of Meiklejohn's outlook, wrote: "Indeed, Meiklejohn's animosity to the profit motive carried him beyond the exclusion of commercial speech from the first amendment."[26]

Still, it was Meiklejohn's regard for listeners' rights, put in a totally different context to be sure (one that emptied the democratic substance of the concept), that provided the rationale for the far-reaching extension of corporate power.

Freedom to engage in political and commercial speech, accorded to corporations in the Court decisions of the 1970s, culminated in the *Bellotti* ruling. It completed the legal framework that now permits, actually encourages, history's most powerful aggregations of economic resources to augment their economic strength with an informational capability. In this era, this capability confers enormous additional power.

The Consequences of *Bellotti*

Exercise of power in the pre-World War II period did not necessitate corporate constitutional speech privilege, though there is little doubt that the money interest rarely lacked the support and endorsement of the press. In general, control of the job market, ownership of machinery and material, and privileged access to government served more than adequately to maintain the corporate domination of the social realm. These means have not lost their efficacy today. Increasingly, however, they require supplementation in the ideological sphere— oversight of what people think and think about.

To achieve this oversight, the informational terrain must be mastered. Such mastery includes, at the outset, the capability to define what the issues are. Next there is the task of framing the issues to meet the objectives of those who do the defining. Finally, ideological mastery necessitates access to information and as complete control as possible over the informational flows coursing through business-, government-, and public-sector channels.

Bellotti et al. enabled corporations to deploy their immense resources and assert hegemonic authority over the informational landscape. The unwillingness of the Court to differentiate between billion-dollar corporations and individuals allows power to be exercised brazenly in the national and local arenas of speech, expression of ideas, and social policy-making. It is a foregone conclusion that the corporate "speaker" will be the "loudest voice in the town."[27] One analysis of *Bellotti* summed it up this way:

> The implications of *Bellotti* are abundantly clear. The assets of corporations may be used for all types of political (public) expression, without regard to whether the content of that expression affects the firms. And that is so even though some corporate behemoths, such as *A.T.&.T.* or *General Motors,* have assets that not only dwarf those of any natural person but also are larger than most nation-states of the world. To pretend that a corporation is a person is a person is a person—to paraphrase Gertrude Stein—and then to proceed that *A.T.&.T.,* for example, is the same as a natural person is to be willfully blind.[28]

Bellotti, the same writer concluded, ". . . was deliberately aimed at enhancing corporate power, and with the obvious secondary consequence of diminishing the power of the individual *qua* natural person."[29]

Not unexpectedly, what was happening in the courts found additional support from the governmental administrative machine. The primacy given to market forces by the Reagan administration since 1980 provided further impetus to the extension of corporate speech. The Federal Communication Commission's abandonment in the period of its mandate to protect the public's interest in broadcasting, for example, nicely complemented the newly increased opportunities for expression presented to the corporate sector by the courts.

Confirming the use to which the *Bellotti* ruling has been put, one study found that "advocacy advertising [corporate editorializing] on television by corporations and private organizations has exploded [since 1980]." "By conservative estimate . . . ," the same study found, "these interests spent $1.8 billion in 1985 to communicate their ideas on various public policy issues. That figure is rising by 10 to 15 percent a year."[30] This comes on top of what are estimated to be 5000 corporate advertising messages a day directed to the public—35,000 a week, 150,000 a month, and almost 2 million over the course of a year.[31]

And yet this may be only the tip of the corporate-message iceberg. A vast and hardly identified, much less examined, number of nonattributed corporate public-relations handouts are being inserted into general television (and undoubtedly other) programming. "Unlike straight advertising," one account informs, "these products of high-tech public relations, designed and distributed to promote a client's interests, are news stories that blend smoothly into the programs."[32] It is believed that some of the more successful video inserts are seen by up to twenty million viewers. When questioned about these practices, the regulatory agencies say "they have little jurisdiction over public relations as opposed to actual advertising [over which they do almost nothing], and that imposing controls could raise freedom-of-speech questions."[33]

Undeniably, *Bellotti* and other recent Court decisions have allowed the corporate sector greater opportunity to exercise influence in the particular environment of the information-using society. Yet the underlying assumptions in these rulings that "modernize" the use of the First Amendment follow closely older conceptions of the economic order. In this, they are at one with the Court's historical position, i.e., that the defense of private property is the primary obligation of the judicial system.

In *Bellotti* and immediately antecedent corporate-speech cases, advertising, for example, is given increasing constitutional protection on the basis of neoclassical economic doctrine that was flawed—as well as partisan to capital—at the time of its original formulation in the late nineteenth century. This is the argument: "A commercial advertisement is constitutionally protected," former Justice Powell wrote for the Court majority in *Bellotti,* "not so much because it pertains to the seller's business as because it furthers the societal interest in the 'free flow of commercial information.' "[34]

Why the "free flow of commercial information" furthered the "societal interest," was explained in another earlier, important commercial-speech ruling, *Virginia Board of Pharmacy.* Writing for the Court majority in that case, Justice Blackmun gave this view of the social utility of advertising:

Advertising . . . is nonetheless dissemination of information as to who is producing and selling what product, for what reason, and at what price. So long as we preserve a predominantly free enterprise economy, the allocation of our resources in large measure will be made through numerous private economic decisions. It is a matter of public interest that those decisions, in the aggregate, be intelligent and well-informed. To this end, the free flow of commercial information is indispensable. And if it is indispensable to the proper allocation of resources in a free enterprise system, it is also indispensable to the formation of intelligent opinions as to how the system ought to be regulated or altered.[35]

The Court's notion of economic decision-making—taken from conventional economics texts—assumes a competitive market of individual buyers and sellers, a free flow of relevant economic information, and the absence of monopoly power. Certainly in current circumstances, and no less in most nineteenth-century economic activity, this model bears slight resemblance to reality. To mention but one of the missing elements, what is to be made of the billion-dollar-plus annual advertising budget of a consumer-goods-producing corporation like Proctor and Gamble? To believe that these mechanisms of the contemporary corporate consumer economy contribute to "intelligent and well-informed decisions," to say nothing of providing socially beneficial allocations of resources, demands fatuous credulity. Advertising, treated as commercial speech and invested with First Amendment rights, enables giant private economic entities, in direct proportion to their command of resources, to shape national economic activity as well as national consciousness. The needs of individuals—*actual* individuals—hardly are congruent with the goals of billion-dollar companies.

Corporate-Speech Rights Versus Social Accountability

First Amendment rights increasingly have been claimed by corporations (whatever their main economic activity). Corporations in the media field, though not newspaper enterprises, are particularly intent in securing this privileged status because it exempts them from social accountability and obligation. The cable-television industry, for example, has intensified its efforts to be considered a legitimate candidate for First Amendment protection, to be treated no differently from the press.

Cable's unqualified free-speech rights have been supported by some scholars, one of whom, the late Ithiel de Sola Pool, expressed the idea in the title of his book, *The Technologies of Freedom*. According to Pool and others, the new electronic technologies, of which cable is a prime example, afford greatly expanded opportunities for communication. This broadened capability, in Pool's opinion, eliminates the need for oversight and regulation. The more than sufficient number of channels will guarantee ample diversity and the justification for regulation is obviated. (Pool was willing to concede that regulation may have been necessary when channel scarcity existed.)

Leaving aside the already well-advanced concentration in the cable industry—wherein a few companies now account for a good part of the national subscribing audience—the fact that cable television indirectly utilizes a public resource, the radio spectrum, does not impress the advocates of cable's constitutional rights. Thus, cable-TV companies have been challenging on First Amendment grounds the authority of municipal governments to grant exclusive franchises for cable delivery and to require cable companies to pay franchise taxes, wire poor neighborhoods as well as rich ones, and set aside channels for public access.[36] These are the social commitments that the cable industry hopes to avoid by seeking First Amendment free-speech rights. It would use this protection to argue that its freedom of speech would be denied or impaired if it is compelled to satisfy the municipal requirements.

Yet the local community, in fact, is the victim if access channels are unavailable. One legal commentator explains the significance of these channels:

> The time has come to update the public forum to the television age . . . television has become America's primary medium language. Use of the streets and parks for expression without the assistance of telecommunications facilities is only partially effective and does not adequately serve the goals of the First Amendment. If society is to attain those goals through television, it cannot rely solely on the commercial media. Rather, channels should be opened for public use: the screen must become the modern town square . . . a general right of affirmative citizen access to cable television has become a practical and constitutional necessity.[37]

Should the cable industry's efforts to put its First Amendment rights—if it is accorded them—above the genuine freedom of speech of the community succeed, the benefits of "the wired city" will never materialize. A designation more appropriate, then, will be "the barbed wire city,"—a place that limits or excludes public expression entirely.

Corporate Speech in the Time Ahead

Expanded corporate-speech doctrine and practice cannot be regarded as completed and irreversible developments, having come into existence only in the last twenty-five years and still evolving. Judicial accordance of First Amendment rights to corporate expression has paralleled the growing role of information in the economy, and especially, its vital importance to corporate business. Yet the structural changes in the economy that have facilitated the substantial growth of corporate speech in recent years have produced another dynamic as well—one which could serve to slow down, and possibly reverse, the corporate-speech express. This is widespread popular opposition to saturated exposure to the corporate message. Already apparent in some instances in the domestic sphere, the opposition is no less evident in the international arena.

The forces which have promoted U.S. economic, military, and cultural preeminence in the post-World War II years began to be exhausted in the early 1970s. Since that time, the American economic position has weakened markedly. Countervailing pressures on U.S. power have emerged. U.S. policy efforts to apply the First Amendments' free-speech provisions to the global activities of U.S. media companies are less and less effective. To be sure, the First Amendment is without standing in international affairs, but it has been invoked all the same, at least in a public-relations manner, to challenge foreign national measures that limit the profitable overseas operations of American media corporations, e.g., import quotas on films and television programs, regulation of foreign advertising, subsidies to domestic cultural-informational productions. This self-serving policy has met growing skepticism and increasing rejection.

Realistically, the application of the doctrine of corporate speech to the international economy is dependent solely on the power that the United States wields in global affairs. The doctrine has no intrinsic value as a universalistic principle, however strongly the corporate-governmental leadership extols it. If and as U.S. power diminishes, corporate speech exercised internationally must rely on the strength of the enterprise expressing itself. U.S. power will be incapable of sustaining it.

This does not necessarily foretell the twilight of corporate expression in the international economy in the immediate future. To the extent that the world system continues to be driven by transnational enterprise (as is currently the situation), corporate speech, especially advertising, will remain an integral part of the system. In fact, the worldwide expansion of advertising continues to be a significant feature of the current period.

At home, the future of corporate speech is no less bound up with the destiny of the economy and how it reacts to the multiple crises affecting it. The consumer society, promoting and depending on continually higher personal levels of consumption, appeared in its mature state after World War II. With this phenomenon came also a great expansion in general education and, with it, the growth of a large professional class. Today, the consumer society is supported by the purchasing power of millions of professionals, supplemented with staggering infusions of personal credit, extolled and driven forward by torrents of advertising across all media.

Yet it is a sign of the vulnerability and fragility of this economy that its legitimating and central ideological force—advertising—is itself the focus of growing (though still limited) dissatisfaction. The implications of this kind of general disaffection for corporate speech are immense. Tens of millions of people, while enjoying a high material standard of living and straining to maintain and extend it, experience deep concerns and growing anxiety over the quality of life that is inextricably connected to the consumer society. In this context, advertising/commercial speech, the lifeline of the consumer society, is being specifically singled out for criticism. The charges are not yet so broad and inclusive that the image-producing industry is threatened seriously. Nor can this disturb for the present overall system equilibrium. Given the centrality of marketing to the consumer society, however, even the stirrings of public dissatisfaction take on significance.

Children's TV and the advertising that constitutes an integral part of it, for example, are periodically castigated. A commentary in a business publication (no voice of extremism) decries the "deteriorating quality of children's (TV) shows in recent years and suggests that government intervention is required."[38] Indeed, the mindless content of most of the programming and the volume of hucksterism foisted on the young viewers arouse widespread indignation despite placebo assurances from TV executives.

The customary corporate response to parental protest is to throw the ball back into the family court, insisting that it is the parents' responsibility to monitor and direct their childrens' viewing. Of course, this is the standard corporate prescription for all social problems—assign responsibility to individuals and families to meet the social disorders produced largely by out-of-control corporate enterprise.

In 1988, the growing public indignation with the quality of childrens' television prompted some attention in Congress. But the matter has not yet become a serious political issue.

Tobacco Advertising: The Achilles Heel
of Corporate Speech?

A more recent challenge to advertising, and one with the potential for recasting the entire issue of corporate-speech rights, has been the effort—unsuccessful to date—to ban totally tobacco advertising. This is no inconsequential economic matter. Tobacco companies in 1986 spent almost three billion dollars on advertising and promotion.[39]

The campaign has received strong support from the medical and legal professions, though a proposal to ban was rejected by the American Bar Association in early 1987. Predictably, "opponents of the proposal [to ban]—(the tobacco industry, newspaper and magazine publishers, and some civil libertarians) said an advertising ban would violate the First Amendment's guarantee of free speech."[40] Corporate speech—in this instance promoting a product that has been scientifically certified to be a serious health hazard—for the time being continues to receive some constitutional sanction. Yet it is also evident that this is an issue that has not been finally settled and could easily extend to the general question of the legitimacy of corporate-speech rights.

At the very minimum, the impact of this particular kind of corporate speech (tobacco advertising) may be stoking the fire for a much more sustained attack, internationally as well as domestically. This has much to do with the groups to whom recent tobacco advertising is directed. In the United States, while the sale of cigarettes to the professional and middle classes declines, the tobacco industry pursues a vigorous campaign to target the less well-protected groups at home and abroad to compensate for this lost revenue. "Tobacco companies," it is reported, "are spending more money to induce blacks to buy their product at a time when the industry is under continued attack. . . . "[41] Cigarette ads on billboards in black neighborhoods proliferate. Black publications are filled with cigarette promotions.

The situation abroad is strikingly similar. Export sales of American cigarettes approximate $2.5 billion annually, and tobacco sales to Asia rose by 76 percent in 1987. At the same time, Korea, Taiwan, China, and even Japan are being swamped with tobacco advertising. In Tokyo, "some doctors say the advertisements we have every night are an assault, like the old B-29 bombings."[42]

How long will life-threatening corporate speech be tolerated and actually defended as an individual, constitutional right? Only as long as the beneficiaries of this kind of expression—the corporate advertisers and the media in which they place their messages—retain sufficient national and international support for their activities.

In Canada, the bell already has tolled. The Canadians, in June 1988, banned all tobacco-products advertising in all media, and after 1993, all billboard and other outdoor advertising will be prohibited as well. More sweeping still, and of great potential impact on the American scene, "the Canadian laws will also ban use of tobacco brand names in connection with cultural and sporting events which have become a major promotional vehicle for the tobacco industry."[43]

In the United States, a many-sided effort is being undertaken by tobacco companies and the advertising industry in general to persuade the public that freedom is endangered if their promotions are restricted. The Philip Morris Company, for example, a giant multinational tobacco and other consumer-goods firm, utilized academic and literary publications to announce an essay contest it was sponsoring in 1987. "Is Liberty Worth Writing For?" its ad inquires. Directly beneath this headline, the First Amendment is reprinted. The ad states further:

> The First Amendment has been a preoccupation of writers and scholars, journalists and politicians for the last 200 years. It has also drawn the grateful attention of business leaders because it promised that the flow of information about legally sold goods and services would not be infringed by government.

> The men and women of Philip Morris believe in the principles set forth in the First Amendment and rise to defend its long-standing application to American business. We believe that a tobacco advertising ban, currently under consideration in Congress, is a clear infringement of free expression in a free market economy.

In this pronouncement, it is noteworthy that a multi-billion-dollar corporation personalizes itself as "the men and women of Philip Morris." A more accurate description would have been "the chief executive officer and the major shareholders of Philip Morris." The instructions for the essay contestants lists these requirements:

> To write an essay of 2500 words or less that explores and questions censorship of expression, in any sector of American life; that defines and defends the First Amendment's application to American business and that specifically questions the ramifications of a tobacco advertising ban on the future of free expression in a free market economy.[44]

Sponsoring an essay contest on the desirability of corporate speech may be viewed as taking "the high road" in persuading the public that smoking ads are part of the heritage of freedom. Philip Morris travels the low road as well. The company, in pursuit of its First Amendment freedom to advertise a carcinogenic product and to forestall a congressional bill that would ban all tobacco advertising, mailed out to hundreds of newspaper editors and media executives copies of *Pravda,* the Soviet newspaper. Across each copy, it made this statement:

> Pravda does not carry cigarette advertising, or indeed any advertising. Government control of information is typical of totalitarian regimes and dictatorships.[45]

One more time, the familiar tactic is employed—to label as "communist" any effort to safeguard the public interest against potentially injurious corporate practice.

Traveling further along the low road, Philip Morris was discovered to have secretly financed ads against banning smoking that were ostensibly paid for by a union. "Full-page newspaper advertisements yesterday (September 22nd, 1987) that opposed a proposed smoking ban on the Long Island Rail Road and Metro-North, were signed by a transit union president, but secretly paid for by Philip Morris."[46]

Corporate Speech Versus the Sovereign State of Florida

Marketing tobacco products is not the only activity in which corporate advertising has become a national issue. In Florida, a state tax on services (which included advertising) was passed by the legislature and scheduled to take effect in mid-1987. It quickly encountered a storm of objection from advertising, consumer-goods corporations and media interests. Especially concerned that this kind of a tax could set a precedent for other states, the vice president for advertising at Proctor and Gamble Co., the world's second largest advertiser (an estimated $1.3 billion in 1986), stated: "If Florida becomes a precedent . . . it would cost the company between $50 [and] $100 million annually."[47]

In defense of their profits, corporate sponsors, advertisers, and the media undertook a campaign of threats, denunciation, and actions against the Florida tax. These included a boycott of Florida for conventions, blacked out programming from Floridian TV screens, and general media vituperation against the tax and its supporters. All of this proceeded under the argument that the tax "is a violation of First Amendment guarantees of speech."[48] If nothing else, the concerted corporate opposition to the tax demonstrated convincingly whose was the loudest voice in the state. The original popular support for the tax was wiped out, the *Wall Street Journal* reported, " . . . apparently due, in part, to a ferocious anti-tax campaign by national advertising groups and others. Most of the state's major media outlets, which suffered ad-revenue losses because of the tax, have campaigned editorially against it . . . nearly a dozen consumer-products companies withdrew ads from Florida media."[49]

Six months after approving the tax on advertising and professional services, the Florida legislature voted to repeal it. The chairman of the Florida House Appropriations Committee summed up the legislature's encounter with the corporate-speech lobby: "Maybe we should just admit we've been beaten to our knees by Wall Street and Madison Avenue."[50]

The National Security State Versus Corporate-Speech Rights

The excesses of corporate advertising and the unwillingness of the advertising and media industries to accept any social accountability are producing public reactions, admittedly still weak, that eventually could be an obstacle to the remarkable advances achieved for corporate speech in recent decades.

More problematic but no less significant, the reining in of commercial speech could come from another direction as well in the time ahead. In a closely divided decision (5–4), the Supreme Court ruled in 1986 that the Commonwealth of Puerto Rico was entitled to restrict local advertising of casino gambling, though the Court allowed the same advertising to be published/broadcast on the U.S. mainland.[51] The rationale of the majority in the Court seemed to be that it was permissible to attract outsiders (mainland U.S. residents) to Puerto Rico's casinos, but it was also within the purview of Puerto Rican state power to deny that opportunity to Puerto Ricans. In dissent, Justice William J. Brennan charged the majority of "dramatically shrinking the scope of the First Amendment protection available to commercial speech, and giving government officials unprecedented authority to eviscerate constitutionally protected expression."[52]

Advertising Age, trade journal of the industry, understandably was deeply troubled by the 1986 Supreme Court ruling. It quoted a Washington lawyer: "There are two recurring themes in [Chief Justice] Rehnquist's votes; one is that corporations have no First Amendment rights. The second is that commercial speech is unprotected and ought to be. He would go back to the 1930s and '40s when any advertising could be banned."[53]

Indeed, why would a deeply conservative justice rule against the interests of the corporate sector in fundamental matters that affect profits, systemic ideology, and economic stability in favor of state regulatory power? The only answer that remotely makes sense is that, to at least some conservative minds, state power provides the sole means of dealing with perceived deep social malaise—crime, pervasive drug use, illegal immigration, "terrorism," and social dissatisfaction in general ("subversion"). The increasingly troubled nature of American society strongly suggests that this line of reasoning (supportive of state power) may be invoked to uphold a disturbingly large range of repressive acts by the state.

The perspective of the right-wing Heritage Foundation is not without relevance here. In the report it prepared for the guidance of the newly elected Reagan administration in 1980, heavy emphasis was placed on "the reality of subversion." "It is axiomatic," the study noted, "that individual liberties are secondary to the requirement of national security and internal civil order."[54] Less pointedly, though more specifically, Robert Sherrill writes: "he [Rehnquist] may be on the right side for the wrong reasons: perhaps he does not abhor corporations (the right reason) so much as he loves the state too much."[55]

Turning to the other side of the argument, the defense of advertising as protected commercial speech—Justice Brennan's view—fortifies and further promotes the already awesome aggregation of private power along with its capability of drowning out alternative views and outlooks.

In either case, we are left with a wrenching set of alternatives—either to accept and defend a further extension of an already pervasive corporate expression or to insist on state restraint of that private capability and thereby contribute to the danger that such restraint may bring with it, i.e., the possibility of excessive and arbitrary state power. Perhaps in a period in which the shocks of rapid techno-social change, propelled almost exclusively by market forces, are tearing apart the social fabric and buffeting individuals unmercifully, it is too much to expect to find neat alternatives and orderly arrays of social choices. The dilemma inherent in this particular choice, between private-corporate and state power, seems resolvable only as a political issue.

As important and powerful as private capital and the state are, there is a third, potentially more decisive force. It has been called "people power." It is the American people, ultimately, who will have to decide. If, in fact, the people's will and awareness—an enormous "if"—are brought to bear on the political process, the bridling of corporate speech need not be the first step toward the abridgement of individual rights and liberties. Actually, these rights and liberties could be expanded as corporate power is forced to retreat. These are not easily realized expectations. They depend on developing the political consciousness, which, in turn, minimally requires a new dimension of media access for those who are now systematically excluded. Do sufficient human resources still exist for this to occur?

Corporate media utterance is but one element—important as it is—in what can be regarded as corporate speech. The extension of corporate influence and control over what was once the public information sector also must be taken into account. It is the focus of the next chapter.

| 4 |

Privatization and Commercialization of the Public Sector: Information and Education

Much of the great American economic expansion in the early postwar years occurred in industries long concentrated and nationally powerful. After the war, firms in these industries grew larger still. Their operations were internationalized. Their corporate voices became stronger and more frequently expressed.

A somewhat different pattern is observable in the growth of a new information industry in the same period. The corporate aggrandizement of the information sector has not been exclusively an outcome of fabulously expanded wealth and assets. These, to be sure, certainly have played a part in the process. But another quite different development also has contributed significantly to the information industry's forward march. This has been the assault on the public sector, the nonprofit, mostly government-administered sphere. In this area, the information-cultural component has suffered most.

Though evident in many measures adopted by Congress before 1980, it was the Reagan administration's policy to gut the public sector. The huge tax reductions in 1981–82, accompanied by the staggering increase in military expenditures, created the mountainous deficits of the 1980s—a trillion dollars of debt piled up in eight years. In the face of these unprecedented deficits, the deep cuts that were made in social and public expenditures were made to seem unavoidable. This, in fact, was the intention of the policy from its inception.[1]

The diminution of public expression and influence that can be found is not the consequence of a decline in national creativity or some other organic disability. It is the result of deliberate and successful efforts to reduce, even eliminate, the public realm in favor of the corporate sector. How this has been accomplished in the informational sphere and the institutional changes that were required to effect the change are the subject of this chapter.

Place of the Informational Sector in the Immediate Postwar Period

The situation in the informational sphere at war's end was quite different than that in the heavy industries. There were no giant companies presiding over the generation, organization, and distribution of information. There were a few large firms producing business calculating equipment. There were also some sizable media corporations. But the production of raw data and processed information, on which businesses have come to depend, were the responsibility of public bodies and government agencies.

The U.S. Bureau of the Census was housed in the Department of Commerce. Every ten years it collected a massive amount of information about people and their demographic condition. There were other similar information-gathering and -generating agencies, most of them in the federal government. Most notable were those in the Agriculture, the Labor, the Treasury, and the Interior departments. There was, in addition, a substantial network of federal research laboratories.

The research labs of the major universities were another source of new information as were the activities of innumerable voluntary and nonprofit organizations. Business carried on research and development too, but a great part of it was for product innovation and improvement. It was also proprietary information.

Most of the information and data produced remained in government stockpiles and archives. Much of it was transferred and made available to the public at national (federal) library depositories scattered around the country.

There was significant government publication activity as well. It centered around, but was not limited to, the Government Printing Office (GPO). The GPO processed and printed many congressional hearings, reports, and departmental studies. Most of these were distributed to the Federal Library Depository System. Ordinarily, interested individuals and businesses could obtain the material fairly easily.

In sum, a good part of the information field a half century ago was an orderly, routinized, and largely governmental sphere of activity. It was not particularly exciting. All the same, it constituted a vital component of the public sector. Individuals could access great masses of information if they had such an interest. Depending on the locale and character of the specific library, more or less of the information stockpile would be available.

With a few exceptions, little money was to be made in the information field. Government materials could not be copyrighted. Accordingly, commercial publishers, for the most part, were not interested in issuing books or manuals that were published originally as government documents. These were available for the asking at a modest price. Commercial publishing itself was, by comparison with the rest of American industry and in contrast to its current state, a quiet, almost cottage, industry. Author-editor relationships were often personal. Paperback publishing was minimal. The million-dollar-book auction was still unknown. The textbook division of publishing was nowhere near the profit center it has become since the numbers of students in higher education skyrocketed after the war.

The marginality of most information enterprise until not much more than a quarter of a century ago was epitomized by its substantial nonprofit, social-service character. Indicative of the low esteem in which most informational work was then held and the prevailing sexism, the library profession—the national nodal point of informational activity—was considered a woman's profession. This meant that the profession's employees were poorly paid and frequently ridiculed in popular-culture stereotypes. Given the relative unimportance and the second-class status of the information field until quite recently, its current prominence and centrality in the general economy are striking.

Still more striking is the actual impact of the elevated importance of information on the country's cultural condition. The increased value placed upon information and *the way this has been expressed* are affecting profoundly most social transactions, nationally and locally.

One way these developments may best be examined and understood is to review the recent history of the American library system and its professional code of service. These are illuminating not because the library has become a political or economic powerhouse in

America. On the contrary, the library, with regard to resource availability at least, has been a puny institution. But libraries historically
have been associated with information collection, organization, and
dissemination. The principles which have governed library practice
may be used as a standard against which to assess the new arrangements that have come to prevail in recent years. Specifically, *the
fundamental principle of American librarianship has been free and
equal access to all users*. This principle has served as a democratic
bulwark. The library, for all its marginality, represented and put into
at least limited practice the democratic aspirations of the nation.

What are the reasons for the greatly enhanced role and value of
information, why has this value forced changes in basic library principles and services, and what are the effects of these developments in
the economy at large and in the cultural sphere in particular?

Developments in the Generation, Transmission, and Use of Information Since the Second World War

The libraries, no less than the national economy, have been deeply
affected by three historically significant and interactive developments
over the last forty years: enormous expansion of scientific and technical information, computerization, and the preeminence of the transnational corporation. There has been an explosive increase in scientific and technological information since the Second World War.
Enormous federal outlays during the war for research and development[2] led to the creation of powerful computers. These expenditures
also created the infrastructure of the governmental-scientific complex
that would be maintained and strengthened in the postwar years.[3] In
the interval between 1960 and 1978, for example, over 400 billion
federal dollars were spent on research and development (R&D).[4] In
1987, not taking into account inflation since 1978, U.S. R&D expenditures totaled $56.1 billion, and the estimate for 1989 amounts to $62.5
billion.[5] These are *federal* expenditures. In recent years, *private* corporate outlays have roughly equalled the government's. The *total* annual R&D outlay currently well exceeds $100 billion.

Since 1945, and with cumulative impact, the amount of information
and data acquired from these heavy outlays has been stupendous. Not
surprisingly, one of the most pressing needs of the engineering, scientific, and administrative sectors is for convenient, rapid, and efficient
access to this vast data supply. Access, in turn, is dependent on the

organization of the material and the availability of suitable means of retrieval and dissemination.

Numerous official commissions were appointed in the postwar years to consider what were termed scientific and technical information (STI) issues. A review of the work of these panels indicates how much attention was given to these problems. A report prepared for the National Science Foundation in 1976, the Mitre Report, listed thirteen major studies between 1958 and 1976 on scientific and technical information issues.[6] Each of these, in varying degree, agreed that STI was a very important sector; that STI is "big business"; that the stakes are very high; and, most pertinently, that severe STI handling problems existed. The Mitre Report quoted a 1969 study by the National Academy of Sciences-Engineering—referred to as the SATCOM report. It noted:

> . . . the proliferation of useful research together with the burgeoning increase in the numbers of trained people involved in science and technology has overcome the capacity of the classical information services to respond effectively. To avert a crisis of major proportions, the only present alternative is a strong effort to accelerate the utilization of modern computer-aided techniques for handling information.[7]

The Mitre Report, and the studies it reviewed, considered the growing national information output as essentially an STI problem. Yet it was not long before it came to be seen in more comprehensive terms as an issue of *general* information abundance and access.

An Arthur D. Little report in 1978 concluded that STI should be regarded as general systemic information. "STI—has to be supplemented with society-related objective information to provide a more complete universe, including economic, demographic, political, occupational, health, legal, regulatory, sociological, cultural environmental information, etc. We call the expanded information set Scientific-Technical and Societal Information (STISI)."[8] In a word, the outpouring of information in the country extended beyond scientific and technical data. It included information about the entire social organism, thereby constituting a still greater challenge for its effective organization and management.

While the growing information and data stockpile provoked a flood of studies and recommendations—among which was the recurrent demand for a national information policy—a technological development was proceeding simultaneously, one which appeared to supply a providential answer to the information explosion.

The Computer and the Emergence
of the Information Industry

Developed during the war into an operational, if still somewhat cumbersome, instrument, the computer was undergoing continuous and rapid technical refinement and capability enhancement. As one generation of computer succeeded another, the size and cost decreased substantially while the processing capacity expanded greatly. Unevenly but rapidly, computers were installed in many branches of the economy. They handled special functions of industrial and governmental operations such as payrolls, personnel records, and inventories. The federal government, banking, and insurance were the first heavy users, shifting the bulk of their transactional business to the new instrumentation. Relatively early, major libraries also found computerization especially useful for their varied informational activities.

What the computer can do with information is still being demonstrated. Its capability to store, organize, rearrange, array, and retrieve data improves from one model to another. These new means of treating and processing data, taken together, mean that specific, practically custom-made information/data can be called up to facilitate the solution of countless problems, projects, and designs. Professionals in law, engineering, the physical and social sciences, the arts, trade, commerce, finance, and, not least, the military, have vastly enhanced work capabilities with the computer.

In a very short time, data, if organized, accessible, and capable of being provided in manipulable and discrete units, became valuable. More compelling still, processed data's contribution to profit-making industrial production and service activities made the data itself a valuable good.

The commercial potential of these new informational possibilities was quickly seen. It led in a few short years to the creation of an information industry whose firms produce, process, package, distribute, and retail information products and services such as legal decisions and texts, commodity and stock prices, specialized industrial statistics, government legislation, and increasingly sophisticated programs for business and individual computer use. The hardware producers make up a different but related and powerful component of the information industry. A study by the American Federation of Information Processing Societies (AFIPS) gives an idea of the speed of these developments:

The computer manufacturing and services industries have grown steadily since 1971; estimated revenues approximately doubled in the five-year period ending 1976 and are forecast to again double in the 5-year period ending 1981.[9]

Heralding the emergence of a new and dynamic sector of the economy, an Information Industry Trade Association (IIA) was established in 1968. Its members included the big information companies such as Dun & Bradstreet, McGraw Hill, and Dow Jones as well as smaller, newly formed firms which packaged and sold data. The formation of the IIA signaled the beginning of a sustained and powerful drive to "promote the development of private enterprise in the field of information and . . . gain recognition for information as a commercial product."[10] The IIA and the industry have pursued this goal tenaciously. In doing so, they have intervened increasingly in national information policy and decision-making.

Information companies are no different than private firms in other sectors in their singleminded objective to engage in profitable enterprise. In the informational field, they advocate and promote a private and commercial context for the outputs that either derive from or can be utilized by a computer-driven economy. Commonplace as this objective of profitability may seem, in the informational sector it is producing consequences that are changing radically the American social landscape. At the same time, it is creating an environment in which information issues that deeply affect the quality of national cultural life are decided by commercial, mostly corporate, considerations.

As computerization and information processing extend throughout the economy, the influence of the for-profit information companies widens. Decisions over the production, organization, storage, and dissemination of information are considered and decided upon without the presence of the public and its representatives. The for-profit information industry's views and interests receive preponderant attention and support, and the business of for-profit information companies grows apace. In the U.S. Department of Commerce's *Industrial Outlook,* it was reported in 1986:

900 firms were responsible for generating revenues of $1.9 billion in the electronic database industry in 1985 (with an estimated growth to 2.2 billion in 1986). 2600 databases were available online, compared to 362 in 1977. The number of customers served by online vendors totalled 784,900 in 1984 compared to 17,000 in 1977.[11]

These numbers already are large understatements of the industry's growth. During 1987, for example, 468 new data bases went online, and as of the beginning of 1988, there were a total of 3,700.[12]

The Private Corporation in the Postwar Years

A third factor accounting for the great increase in the importance of information has been the striking growth of the private corporation, already substantial in prewar days. Today, a large and growing share of the global output of goods and services comes from the activities of some thousands of transnational companies, many of which are still owned by private U.S. interests. These huge economic entities have become heavily dependent on computers and telecommunications (satellites, cables) in their daily national and global operations. In 1985, the Business Roundtable, an organization comprised of 500 chief executives of the most powerful U.S. companies, highlighted this dependence:

> telecommunications is central to the operations of all multinational business activity . . . (moreover) the dependence of multinational corporations—whether they are pursuing intracorporate functions or providing services or both—upon international information transfer is steadily increasing.[13]

Recapitulating, the emergence of information as a valuable and salable good is founded on massive data production, the availability of computerization, the development of an influential private information industry, and corporate dependence on new information technologies and information flows. In turn, the growing commercialization of information supplies the motor that is radically restructuring the economy and American culture.

The commercial value increasingly attached to information initiates changes that ramify throughout the economy's basic economic and social processes. Two places where this dynamic is clearly at work are the nation's major libraries and the national government's information function. In both places, the intrusion of commercialization is marked.

In 1977, Lee Burchinal, at that time director of the Division of Science Information of the National Science Foundation, assessed the forces that were imposing change in libraries. Speaking at a conference concerned with "the on-line revolution in libraries," Burchinal pointed out that the "driving forces" for the changes taking place in libraries—i.e., "substitution of nonprint form of distribution" and "extensive use of outside services for accessing large remote sources of needed information . . . *lie outside the library field and its on-line suppliers.*" "The main impetus," Burchinal found, "is derived from the dynamics of the major elements comprising the U.S. information economy. Information processing requirements of business, banking, and other commercial enterprises are immense. So are those of the military and civilian sides of the federal government . . . in effect . . . libraries and their on-line suppliers—are following the lead of other industries." Burchinal concluded:

> On-line developments in the library field will not compel rethinking or reformulation of national information policies. But the converse is true—decisions regarding national communication policies and practices will have profound effects on libraries and their operations.[14]

Burchinal emphasized the *passive* nature of the library's interaction with the development of commercialized information. He understood that the provision of electronically transmitted information from commercial vendors was being *imposed* on the library by the forces he outlined above.

But what may have begun as a necessary response to external stimuli has launched a dynamic of its own. The changes that have been occurring in libraries are initiating new ways of how information is and will be organized in the economy overall. The library, as a key institution in the information arena, is by force of circumstance at the vortex of the changes already completed and those still being made.

Relatedly, the institutions that eventually preside over these vital information functions will, in fact, largely determine the tone and character of most social transactions. They will deeply influence as well the world of individual consciousness. Developments in the library sector—the major research libraries mainly but not exclusively—provide a window on some of the profound changes already evident in the national and cultural sphere. These developments have brought into question fundamental library values, if not endangering the survival of the existing library system itself.

The new information technologies with their commercial, profit-making arrangements have been the means of effecting the changes that have occurred in recent years in the nation's main libraries. To defray the costs of the computerization which has been installed to manage the growing stream of information flowing in and the equally large increase in demand for that information, fees for services have been introduced. These were expected to enhance information delivery and enhance the library's role in providing the services. Important and unforeseen effects, however, soon became evident. Some of these were described at a relatively early date in a study of on-line services to university libraries:

> During the initial period, online services, supported in part by user fees (in part by library funding), was often viewed as a single added activity to supplement standard reference service, which would continue to coexist. The interrelationships between the two types of services were recognized, but were not directly visible. The developing shift in library resource allocations from free services to fee services, and with it the redirection of resources from one user population to another was less perceptible. . . .
>
> *The introduction of online services for a fee is not simply an added activity for those who can pay, but represents a reallocation of library resources from one set of activities to another, and from one set of users to another.*[15]

This is a very basic shift indeed. In the reallocation of information resources now occurring *throughout the economy* from one set of users (the general population) to another (mostly corporate business users), one principle prevails. It is the market criterion—the ability to pay. This determines who will receive and who will be excluded from the benefits of the information-lubricated economy. In major libraries, this basic policy decision was accompanied by the imposition of user charges for access to the new electronic systems.[16]

The imposition of user charges in American libraries, understandable in terms of the resource limitations of the library sector, all the same, gave powerful support to the IIA's goal of advancing the commercialization of information. Yet this goal is inherently incompatible with the underlying and historical, if inadequately fulfilled, principle of public library service—*equal access for all* to the nation's informational resources.

Transforming information into a salable good, available only to those with the ability to pay for it, changes the goal of information access from an egalitarian to a privileged condition. The consequence of this is that the essential underpinning of a democratic order is seriously, if not fatally, damaged. This is the ultimate outcome of commercializing information throughout the social sphere. For this reason, though countless important questions confront the American library community and the public information sphere, the issue of commercialization of information is the transcendent question. It affects the future of the nation as well as that of the nation's libraries.

How the pressure to commercialize information has compelled accommodation, albeit reluctantly, in American cultural institutions is seen in the record of the soulful wrestling with the issue in the deliberations of the American library community. Given the stakes and taking into account the strengths of the interest groups involved, it was to be expected that the issues of commercial information and the library's connection to the rapidly growing private information industry appeared early as perplexing and urgent matters facing the library profession and community.

A Review of the Question of Commercialization and Privatization of Information in the Library Field—1970s to the 1980s

A brief and selective review of the major studies, reports, and proceedings of the American Library Association and related or concerned bodies and commissions reveals the growing pressure from the private information sector. It demonstrates as well the resistance to this pressure displayed by the American library community.

In 1975, as the economy's utilization of advanced information technology was moving into high gear, the National Commission on Libraries and Information Science (NCLIS), created in 1970 in the Nixon administration, prepared a report on long-term goals for a national program for library and information services. The counterpressures already were evident. On the basic issue of information equality, the report recommended: ". . . Federal legislation that would adopt as its prime philosophical goal equal opportunity of access to the nation's library and information services."[17] Additionally, ". . . the Federal Government must bear a permanent responsibility for preserving and maintaining the knowledge resources of the nation and for making a specific commitment to their interdependent development."[18]

At the same time, however, the commission urged a major role for the private information industry in organizing and distributing information. It foresaw that "the information industry will exert increased influence on the nation's information services in the years ahead."[19] Acknowledging the industry's already considerable influence, the commission recommended that "greater collaboration should be developed between libraries and the commercial and other private sector distributors of the newer information services when the results are in the public interest."[20] How that determination would be made was left unaddressed!

Reflecting now on NCLIS's mid-1970s study, the commission may have been realistic in conceding a larger role to the for-profit information industry in the country's informational condition. But as became increasingly apparent over time, the information industry was and is interested in collaboration with the public sector only to the extent it can use it for furthering its own objectives. As these have been attained, interest in collaboration wanes, and the public library sphere contracts. Still, the insistence in the 1975 statement on equal access to information must be regarded as an important reaffirmation of library goals.

A year later, a report prepared by the staff of the Domestic Council Committee on the Right of Privacy, chaired by Nelson Rockefeller, published by the National Commission on Libraries and Information Science, revealed a distinct shift of emphasis. In this report, "public-sector interests" are infrequently mentioned. Information supply is almost totally a commercial consideration. The voice and perspective of the information industry are pervasive. Government (public) information is seen as a preserve to be handed over to private information managers and entrepreneurs.

The report's unabashed private-sector tone and approach were evident. In one section, the problem—as it is seen from the private information industry's standpoint—is stated explicitly. In brief, it is how to "dismantle" the national structure of public information supply and enable private information interests to become its expropriators:

> Some of the most difficult issues facing the government result from the growth of a new commercial information sector in the United States. This new industry often finds itself in conflict with governmental dissemination services. It seeks a resolution of these conflicts and a uniform set of policies that will provide a climate for its growth and investment.

The report explains why this is a problem:

> The problem is complex, since the dissemination of government-generated information is a legal responsibility of the Federal agencies, either specifically written into the agency legislation, or implied in agency mission descriptions. Moreover, many of the information programs of the Federal agencies have grown over the years and have become national and international in scope, making *dismantling* diffi-

cult. Several of the agencies have taken steps to turn some parts of their dissemination programs over to private sector contractors, *but the commercial industry believes this effort to be insufficient.*[21]

In another section, the report presents without endorsing "The For-Profit Sector View," which flatly asserts:

> While publicly supported library functions providing free information should not be abolished, it should be recognized that there is no such thing as *free* information.[22]

In the general discussion, the report's authors see the issue as "how to provide information services to the public and at the same time establish policies that will not *penalize* the commercial information sector."[23]

This report, issued in the waning days of the custodial Ford administration, seemed to be forgotten. But the IIA's views would be more and more forcefully articulated as the industry itself grew in size and influence. In fact, in the mid-1980s, the report's perspectives provided the framework for the decisions for the key agency of the Reagan administration's control of information, the Office of Management and Budget (OMB).

Yet despite the information industry's growing strength, its ability to influence national information policy has not been without opposition. The public's right to equal information access has been defended all along the way. The problem has not been with the sudden abandonment of this principle but in its gradual weakening. This has been done by the adoption of govermental administrative measures and processes which undermine and destroy the social character of information.

The White House Conference on Library and Information Services

The next major library event at which the commercialization of information was an issue was the White House Conference on Library and Information Services, held in Washington, D.C., in 1979. The conference's purpose "was to improve the nation's libraries and information centers and their use by the public."[24] The conference was a landmark in the nation's library and information history. At the meeting, 806 delegates approved sixty-four resolutions which touched on many important informational matters. Among its goals and objectives, the

White House conference approved in general session a resolution on a national policy for free access which read as follows:

> Whereas, information in a free society is a basic right of any individual, essential for all persons, at all age levels and all economic and social levels, and Whereas, publicly supported libraries are institutions for education for democratic living and exist to provide information for all, Therefore, be it resolved, that the White House Conference on Library and Information Services hereby affirms that all persons should have free access, without charge or fee to the individual, to information in public and publicly supported libraries, and Be It Further Resolved, that the White House Conference on Library and Information Services advocates the formation of a National Information Policy to ensure the right of access without charge or fee to the individual to all public and publicly supported libraries for all purposes.[25]

In addition to this unqualified endorsement of free public access to information, the White House conference also recommended that the "United States Congress continue to foster broad public participation in the Federal Government by substantial subsidies on the sale of basic Federal documents and continue to maintain a system of regional and local depositories for Government information."[26]

Steadfast as these resolutions were in their insistence on adherence to the social basis for information provision, the increasingly deregulated economy, and the private information sector in particular, brushed them aside. This was strikingly evident in another report, issued hard on the heels of the White House conference by a task force surprisingly "assembled and funded by the National Commission on Libraries and Information Science (NCLIS)."[27] The subject of the task force's attention was the interaction of the public and private sectors in providing information services. That the library community undertook an examination of this important issue at a relatively early date is worth noting. What came out of the study is another matter. Commissioned in 1979, the report was issued in early 1982.

The *Public/Private Sector Report,* as it has come to be known, can be regarded as signaling the turning point in the struggle for command of the nation's information resources. With the publication of this report, it was clear that the balance had moved decisively toward the commercial information industry and away from the principle of information as a social good. The report may be read as a declaration of the private sector's triumph in the information sphere.[28]

Collaboration between the public and private information sectors was no longer an aim of the industry, as it had been in the 1975 NCLIS report. The Public/Private Sector Task Force, with its hard-to-miss, overrepresented, private-sector membership, acknowledged the changed situation and the new balance of forces favorable to industry:

> . . . Should the sectors be regarded as cooperating in the process of distribution of information? Some members of the Task Force see government and the private sector as cooperating components, each meeting needs of society in the way that it best does; others see them either as competitive, or, at most, complementary, without a pattern of sharing responsibility. *Since many of the previous studies and reports have recommended "cooperation between the public and private sectors," it is especially important to note that this has become an issue of controversy in the Task Force, rather than an accepted truth.*[29]

In fact, in the report private industry challenged the right of the public sector (government, libraries, public universities, etc.) to engage in *any* informational activities the industry regarded as its own province. For example, "The most basic issue of controversy, of course, related to the role of government. . . . It's not so much a matter of 'capitalism vs socialism,' since there seems to be none on the Task Force that would urge that the government should 'take over' any segment of the information industry. It does seem to be a matter of whether or not the government should provide *any* services that could be provided by the non-governmental sector."[30] The report's emphasis throughout is the encouragement of the private sector and the fullest utilization of the market—selling for profit—in the collection, processing, and dissemination of government information. Thus, the trajectory of the private information sector in its interaction with the library community (and whomever else might uphold the principle of equal access to information for all—financed as a social cost) has been from cooperation to unilateral assertion and exclusion.

In recent years, libraries are increasingly being put into the position of adjunct to and facilitator for the commercial information industry. Despite an initial reluctance to become involved in commercial practices—i.e., charging users for information, relying on private vendors for data bases, contracting out functions to private firms, etc.—libraries now almost routinely adopt such practices. Meanwhile, the distinction between a library and a commercial enterprise narrows. The library's options to preserve its vital social role also diminish.

Librarians and libraries who lack enthusiasm for the commercial features of the information age become barriers to the full-scale triumph of privatization in the national information sphere. Given the commercial dynamic at work, the physical elimination of libraries, at least in their customary form, is by no means an outlandish prospect.

The phenomenal increase of personal computers allows the private information industry to anticipate, perhaps overoptimistically, a time in which libraries may be bypassed altogether. Information provision in this projected scenario would be in the hands of private "information professionals" or directly available to individual end-users, naturally at a price!

Already some "bottom-line educators" are wondering whether there is a need for traditional library schools. Who needs librarians, educated according to a social ethic, if information can be supplied by entrepreneurs and private businesses unencumbered by social principles?[31] An opaque word, "disintermediation," is coming into use to obscure a very transparent process by which librarians may lose their jobs in the future.

The changeover now occurring in libraries is not simply a matter of introducing superior techniques and instrumentation which permit all participants in the information arena—providers, users, and the general public—to benefit. Along with the new electronic technologies come a set of arrangements—social relations if you will. These, as they have developed in recent years under the pressure of private interest and deliberate conservative budget-cutting policy, introduce the mechanics of the market to what had been a public sphere of social-knowledge activity.

Compare, for example, the commercial data-base vendor Dialog's motive for acquiring data bases with the library's long-term goal of acquiring as much of the social knowledge of the world as possible—constrained by limited resources, naturally. Dialog's president informs: "We can't afford an investment in databases that are not going to earn their keep and pay back their development costs." Asked what areas currently are not paying their development costs, his answer was: "Humanities."[32]

No less threatening to the public's informational well-being, Dialog in 1987 refused to make available some of its data bases to unions who wanted to use the data in them in their bargaining with management. The data bases withheld were owned by Dun & Bradstreet, one of the largest information companies in the nation. Dun & Bradstreet instructed Dialog not to make the data available. This decision eventually was rescinded because of a public outcry. The attempt, however, hardly inspires confidence.[33]

Privatization and Commercialization of the National Information Supply

By the mid-1980s, the commercialization of information—its purchase and sale under the auspices of an increasingly powerful private information sector—has become the dominant feature of the American information-using economy. In the Reagan years, the views and demands of the information industry have been made into national goals, inscribed in legislation and executive orders, i.e., the Paperwork Reduction Act of 1980, the Office of Management and Budget's Circular A-130 on management of federal information resources (December 12, 1985), and an earlier circular (A-76) dating back to the mid-sixties on using private sector contractors for government functions. These measures have been designed, or interpreted, to establish the primacy and legitimacy of the market over the informational sphere. They also instruct government agencies to yield their information to private firms.

Like McDonald's and Lee Iacocca, the information industry in America seems beyond criticism. The major media are dazzled by surface phenomena: the undeniable technical wizardry of the new electronic systems of data and image projection, the increasing number of jobs that the information industry promises to create, the utilization of sophisticated, "instructed" equipment. Adding to the general bedazzlement is the blinding rapidity with which computers have been installed in government bureaus, commercial offices, and service industries. Artifacts of the information age have become a routine sight—product scanners in supermarkets, cash registers that resemble the control panels of jumbo jets, electronically coded plastic cards instead of room keys for hotels and motels, computer terminals replacing card catalogues in libraries. The commercial utilization of information has become a central force in our society, yet there has been an almost complete absence of discussion of the political and policy issues it raises.

The drive to privatize public information has been enormously facilitated by the Reagan administration's commitment to dismantling the government's social-welfare functions. Privatization has been pursued within the bureaucracy through the Office of Management and Budget, which has been elevated into a superagency. It presides over the plans, programs, and information activities of all the other agencies. Since the early years of the Reagan administration, it has been spearheading the effort to reduce the government's traditional responsibility to collect, compile, and disseminate information.

OMB Watch, a public-interest, nonprofit organization, reports, "Since 1981, OMB has been trying to eliminate most if not all of the federal government's public information services. It not only has restricted agency information activities, but also has attacked the traditional policies and management of government printing. This has meant a direct challenge to the Government Printing Office (GPO) and the congressional Joint Committee on Printing (JCP), which have supervised government printing since 1860."[34]

The person in charge of federal statistical programs for the OMB in the early years of the Reagan administration explained what was behind his agency's cutbacks in gathering and disseminating data. "We hope in the future to make the additional information—[that which was being eliminated]—available to private firms on a user-fee basis."[35] Already, at that time, a consortium of fifteen companies had been formed to purchase specialized data from the Census Bureau. "In the past," it was noted, "the Bureau sold directly to users, for a relatively small fee, a computer tape with special tabulations of census data by zip code. This year (1982) however, the Bureau sold for $250,000 an 18-month exclusive right to the tapes to the consortium, whose members included Sears Roebuck, Montgomery Ward, Time Magazine, and State Farm Insurance Companies. Each member of the consortium will prepare its own tabulations and market them to other users for several times the price the Census Bureau used to charge."[36]

A few years later, in 1986, some of the effects of gutting the public's information supply were (momentarily) observable. A nonpartisan group in Chicago discovered that 34,000 people in Cook County were registered to vote twice. When appraised of this finding, the chairman of the Chicago Board of Election Commissioners acknowledged "that direct-mail companies know more about people than city or county voting authorities."[37]

By OMB edict, many government publications that served the needs of the general public have been discontinued.[38] And the departments of Labor, Commerce, Agriculture, Energy, Health and Human Services, et al., the customary organizers of a large part of the national information supply, are being compelled to justify their statistical data-collection projects to a generally hostile overseer, the OMB.

Meanwhile, private companies are demanding, with the encouragement of the OMB, the right to acquire, organize, and disseminate what they regard as the most profitable items in the national data stockpile. Federal data bases, for example, have been targeted for privatization. How this works out is the focus of one report:

> One private data base already in operation is the Electronic Dissemination of Information (EDI) system at the U.S. Department of Agriculture (USDA). Considered by OMB as a prototype, EDI is owned and maintained by Martin Marietta Data Systems (MMDS) (The parent company, Martin Marietta, is one of the largest defense contractors in the nation). The database maintains and disseminates data compiled by the USDA, at taxpayers expense, including crop reports, press releases, food and nutrition data, agricultural trade data, market reports, and economic and statistical information. . . . The agency (USDA) pays Martin Marietta Data Systems to take this information. What's more . . . Martin Marietta actually sells this information back to the USDA whenever access by the agency is required. MMDS makes the data available to the public by way of its own computer network. Users who wish to obtain information from EDI must pay a fee of $150 per month plus the cost of the special electronic hardware, as well as the 2 to 5 cents per line charge and the long distance and connection charges. . . . Although USDA information is still available in paper copy to the network of 1,400 Federal Depository Libraries for free public access, the USDA hopes to eventually do away with paper altogether.[39]

In this neat arrangement, the public pays twice for information, if it is able to obtain it in the first place. In the process, the public information stockpile is transferred to corporate custody for private profit-making.

Other assaults on the national information supply are multiplying. For example, when the Department of Commerce announced its intentions in 1986 to privatize the National Technical Information Service (NTIS), a clearinghouse for the collection of scientific, technical, and engineering information, it did not ask for comments on the desirability of privatization itself, which was considered a settled issue, but on what form privatization might take. The service's collection of scientific reports and studies from 2,000 sources, both U.S. and foreign, includes an archive of more than 1.6 million titles, which are kept available to scholars and the general public. If privatized, there is no assurance that the flow of materials into the archive would continue, that foreign information would still be available, that infrequently purchased reports would be stockpiled, and that government-produced information would not be copyrighted. The privatization plans for NTIS have been set back. The publicity given to this project created sufficient opposition to compel a different arrangement. But the assault on the public informational sector continues.

The role of the Federal Depository Library Program in collecting and circulating government documents is being undermined by unavailability of these documents. Budgetary constraints have prevented it from acquiring the latest electronic equipment for information delivery. The scholarly riches reposing in the National Archives have been made less available because of funding cutbacks. Federal libraries, which set the standard for libraries across the nation, are starved for funds, and many of their activities have been contracted out to private firms.

Across the nation, the control of existing computerized files established by states and the national government is fiercely contested by the information industry. *Business Week* in mid-1988 reported:

> As the stakes get higher, the data industry is more willing to fight for access. . . . Data companies argue that private information services are more attuned to customers' needs. Besides that, they don't like government competition. . . . [The] Office of Management and Budget sides with industry . . . "We want to warn [government] agencies that they shouldn't be too entrepreneurial," says an OMB official.[40]

Another raid on the national information stockpile, still in the experimental stage, may come in the *initial* phase of data collection. The government has approved pilot programs in which private contractors manage the electronic filing, processing, and dissemination of data that businesses and individuals are required to submit to government agencies and commissions. The data include the more than 100,000 applications that the Patent and Trademark Office receives annually and the disclosure statements that publicly held companies must file with the Securities and Exchange Commission.

These private arrangements raise a host of questions. Will they affect the accuracy and quality of the data? Who will decide what will be stored and what discarded? How will public access to this material be insured? Who owns the data after it is processed by private firms? The answers will be forthcoming in the private practice. There is no cause for confidence that the public interest in what was once public information will be protected.

Privatization of Higher Education
and Commercialization of Research

The commercialization of the public information sector does not halt at the corporate pillaging of the national information supply and the undermining of the library principle and practice of free and equal access for all to information. In the nation's universities, too, the dynamic of information commercialization is at work. "The relationship between academe and business is more cordial than it has been in decades," reports the *Chronicle of Higher Education*. "The sectors are increasingly resembling each other."[41] The crucial connection is information.

Corporations aim to siphon off the findings in the academic laboratories and institutes for their own profit. With few exceptions, administrators of the top schools, squeezed by declining public support, have welcomed corporate offers of money, equipment, laboratories and research facilities, and contributions to the salaries and upkeep of marketable (those doing commercially applicable research) professors.

Reporting that the "line between public and private institutions is blurring in nations throughout the world," a group of distinguished educators in 1987 welcomed the spread of privatization and commercialization in higher education. "The blur is where the action is," stated Harlan Cleveland, dean of the Hubert H. Humphrey Institute of Public Affairs at the University of Minnesota. "When university and industry researchers work together," he noted, "they quicken the pace at which laboratory findings can be put into the marketplace."[42]

Cooperation also quickens the pace at which the marketplace and its rules are moving into the university. The process is well under way. Reporting on "Business-Campus Ventures," the *New York Times* found that "corporations provided an estimated $600 million to universities for research and development in 1986."[43] Among the largest recipients of this corporate expenditure were MIT, Carnegie-Mellon, Georgia Institute of Technology, University of Michigan, Washington University, and the University of Arizona.

Alongside the growing corporate intrusion into potentially high-profit university research areas, a still more direct link has been forged in recent years. The long-standing domination of private-enterprise ideology and assumptions over the entire educational enterprise has been evident for a very long time. However, those institutional arrangements that enable the corporation to undertake a *direct* educational function require further comment.

A Carnegie Foundation special report, aptly titled *Corporate Classrooms: The Learning Business,* informs that American corporations now are spending upwards of $40 billion each year, "approaching the total annual expenditures of all America's four-year and graduate colleges and universities," to train and educate their employees. In 1978, it was reported that "business firms gave in-house training to about 6.8 million trainees."[44]

Individual corporate educational activity is equally impressive. AT&T, according to this account, "performs more education and training functions than any university in the world." IBM invested half a billion dollars in employee education in 1982. It is no surprise to learn that "corporate learning centers are more modern, sleek, and up-to-date than traditional colleges with classrooms. . . . They surpass many universities in their sophistication both in offerings and in the delivery systems as well."[45]

The line between a "corporate learning center" and a university also is blurring, according to the *Chronicle of Higher Education.* In a widely publicized incident in 1987, a Wall Street "takeover expert," teaching a course at the Columbia University Business School, proposed turning his class into a takeover seminar. He would pay the students if they came up with suitable takeover projects that he could exploit, i.e., companies ripe for raiders. In this case, though the project was unassailable as a "learning exercise," it was a little too much for Columbia's administrators. Its crassness offended educators who generally have no problem with the school's goal—making money in the marketplace.[46]

The Damage Thus Far

The American public library and its democratic principles have not disappeared yet. Neither have the country's universities and colleges moved their classrooms into corporate enclosures. The national information supply, derived from censuses, government hearings and studies and reports, federally funded research, etc., continues to be produced, if somewhat diminished and skewed by continuing efforts to appropriate it for private corporate advantage. But the direction and tempo of the changes that are affecting these basic institutions leave no grounds for complacency.

Some might conclude that the developments that have been described in the preceding pages are merely oscillations around a fairly stable and settled public/private-sector equilibrium. However, the extent to which privatization and commercialization already have penetrated the public informational sphere and how threatening this has become are the messages of an extraordinary statement of concern issued in 1985 by the Council on Library Resources, a private, thirty-year-old, Ford Foundation–supported organization.

> Ways must be found to assure continuing attention for those aspects of culture and learning that are important but, in a commercial sense, not necessarily in fashion. . . . Uncritical adherence to the concept of information as a commodity will distort the agendas of institutions and disciplines alike. . . . Public interest in the principle of open access must appropriately influence the structure of the information system and its components. It is certain that the information needs of society cannot be defined by the marketplace alone.[47]

In recent years, the informational-cultural sector has literally been turned over to the marketplace. The breadth of the movement away from public to corporate expression extends across the entire social landscape. It is to some of these developments in the arts, architecture, and the urban scene that we now turn.

| 5 |

The Corporate Capture of
the Sites of Public Expression

In the early nineteenth century, British landlords took over the lands of the Commons—the acreage for use by the entire community—and those of small proprietors as well in a series of acts of enclosure. Enclosure is the appropriate description for what has been happening in the United States in the last twenty-five years, not to farmlands—most of that has long since been bought up by corporate agribusinesses—but to the sites and channels of public expression and creativity. How, for example, are museums utilized; what has been happening to living space itself—in cities and suburbs—and why; and, finally, what factors govern the use of the airwaves—radio broadcasting and television programming. These are all sites of public involvement and can be viewed much like renewable natural resources. They are not exhausted or depleted by use. They provide daily replenishment for the body's physical and emotional needs. If these vital resources are seized for private ends, human health and consciousness itself are held hostage.

Hans Magnus Enzensberger, concerned over what he called "the industrialization of the mind"[1] and the debilitating impact of products of cultural industries on human consciousness, still held out a hopeful prospect. Despite the awful effect of applying the techniques of industrialization to the activity of the mind, there remained, according to Enzensberger, one human quality that the dominant system could not entirely subdue. At the same time, it could not do without it. This is the creativity of individuals, the same creativity that provided the compelling products of the cultural industries.

Enzensberger believed that this creative talent, however much it was harnessed for systemic ends, remained a source of potential resistance and change. Fully aware of the risk of participating, Enzensberger still concluded that there was no way for intellectuals and creative individuals to opt out of the system. Though the consciousness industry—an inclusive term for the many ways in which consciousness is influenced by the products of the cultural industries—preempted everything it came in contact with, he recommended that the creative ones "enter the game . . . take and calculate [the] risks."

The Industrialization of the Mind was written in 1962. Since then the consciousness industry and its many branches have become mighty profit centers—favorite expression of the 1980s—as well as cultural conditioners. Additionally, the corporate order, however much it continues to rely on the creative energies of individuals in the many subdivisions of the cultural industries, also has learned a great deal more about the business of employing the energies of its hired talent to its own ends.

The dialectic that Enzensberger identified and analyzed—the strength of the consciousness industry and, at the same time, its vulnerability—remains operative. But for this historical moment, at least, the strategies and practices of the consciousness industry to maintain the upper hand are in the ascendance. The counterforces are yet to be revealed.

Hardly exaggerated, I believe, are the conclusions in a study of the image creations of one American supercorporation, General Electric. The author finds that

> . . . it is not possible to survey the forms of mass culture in the twentieth century with the assumptions [of the mid-nineteenth century]. The corporation creates patterns of meaning wholesale and sells them to the public. It divides society into markets while ignoring fundamental divisions between workers and white-collar personnel, between regions, and between ethnic groups. The forms of mass culture, including world's fairs, magazines, advertising, corporate photography, commercial radio and television, and public relations, present a systematically controlled image of American society. The forms of communication and the large companies that control them must be linked in any investigation.[2]

Actually, this is an understatement of the breadth of current corporate image and definition control. Enzensberger's review described a still wider category of these activities: ". . . fashion and industrial design, the propagation of established religions and esoteric cults, opinion polls, simulation, and last but not least, tourism, which can be considered a mass medium in its own right."[3] All these branches of the consciousness industry are economically motivated. They are engaged in selling in the market for profit. The trials and antics of Jimmy Swaggart, whose television ministry took in over $120 million a year, make the inclusion of religion more than rhetorical.

What is especially notable about the current period is the entrance of the profit motive into fields which, for different reasons, historically had escaped this now pervasive force. An example of this development is in the field of public information. The determined and increasingly successful efforts to appropriate public (governmental) information for commercial advantage has been noted. In this ongoing development, an entirely new private industry, the information industry, has been created. It is an especially influential addition to the general consciousness industry.

A different approach is observable in the treatment of other public-sector institutions and functions. In many of these, corporate interest is served best by allowing a public-sector activity to survive and possibly to prosper moderately. But while doing so, its function is transformed from service to the public to benefitting the corporate order. In short, the transformed activity, though still ostensibly public, has become a component of the consciousness industry. Nowhere is this more evident than in recent practices in some of the country's important museums.

The Museum as Corporate Showcase

It may seem curious to regard museums as part of the public sector in the first place. Historically, museums generally have not been grassroots institutions. Invariably supported by wealthy patrons and private endowments, the museum usually has served as a reminder and celebrant of the established order, past and present. In the rare instances where some examples of social conflict might be on display, the exhibit could be relied upon to offer a social tableau more appropriate for a cryogenic installation than for current instruction in social change.

If their exhibits were frozen in time, so were their sources of financial support. The museum building itself was customarily a tribute to older fortunes, whose owners' names often prominently adorned the masonry. But such tributes were not advertisements for current enterprises. Also, the museum, for all its moneyed origins, was used as a public resource. Schoolchildren, as part of their public education, frequently came in their classes to museums.

Schoolchildren still visit museums, but there is new management of the premises. It follows a different style and entertains an altogether new objective. The museum has been enlisted as a corporate instrument. It has been made an adjunct to the consciousness industry. At the same time, it maintains the appearance of a public resource and a site of public creative expression.

The transformation of museums into "becoming public relations agents for the interests of big business and its ideological allies"[4] can be dated roughly from the mid-1960s. In that period, the Metropolitan Museum of Art in New York City began its practice of installing temporary exhibitions with huge banners, often indicating the corporate sponsorship, draped in front of the building. These announced the show and offered "spectacle and entertainment" that blended well with the already rampant consumerism in the country.

It must be conceded that the museum is but one institution in the art world. Yet, what can be observed in current practices here constitutes a subset of the larger art world. American corporations spent $22 million on the arts in 1967—most of which did not go to museums. By the end of 1987, the outlay is expected to come close to $1 billion.[5] What accounts for the surge in corporate spending on the arts? Not so long ago, such expenditures would have been derided by hardnosed pragmatists as money down the drain.

Hans Haacke turned his attention, and his artist's sensibility, to this phenomenon early in its development and produced an exhibition in 1975 in New York City which he entitled "On Social Grease." The show, comprised of six plaques of photoengraved magnesium plates mounted on aluminum, reproduced the statements of six national figures (five corporate and one political) on the utility of the arts to business. Robert Kingsley, Exxon executive and founder and chairman of the Arts and Business Council, gave Haacke his exhibition title:

> Exxon's support of the arts serves as a social lubricant. And if business is to continue in big cities, it needs a lubricated environment.[6]

David Rockefeller was more specific:

> From an economic standpoint, such involvement in the arts can mean direct and tangible benefits. It can provide a company with extensive publicity and advertising, a brighter public reputation, and an improved

corporate image. It can build better customer relations, a readier acceptance of company products, and a superior appraisal of their quality. Promotion of the arts can improve the morale of employees and help attract qualified personnel.[7]

In any case, the arts, and the museums, are being well lubricated with corporate sponsorship. Mobil Oil Corporation pays to keep several museums open one night a week and announces its generosity in the press.[8] Not to be outdone, the Chase Manhattan Bank announces that "At Chase, we're committed to enriching lives not only financially, but culturally" and entices the director of the Guggenheim Museum to pose in front of Frank Lloyd Wright's building and wisecrack: "Individual and corporate support has kept us in the black. Not to mention cobalt blue, cadmium yellow, and burnt sienna."[9] And AT&T, acting like a summer hotel activities director, ordered "Everybody into the Met [Metropolitan Museum of Art]" for a David Hockney show it had underwritten.[10]

Each week, the art pages of the *New York Times* carry listings of exhibits and shows in galleries and museums, underwritten by the Philip Morris Company, Inc., an especially big spender on the arts and known also for its heavily advertised cigarettes. In Canada, a law enacted in 1988 expressly forbids this practice. It bans the use of tobacco brand names if they are linked to cultural and sporting events. In America, Philip Morris public-spiritedly calls attention in a two-page, color spread in the *New York Times* to a new exhibition of art in black America at a Harlem museum,[11] while at the same time saturating black neighborhoods, in media targeting black people, with cigarette ads—possibly to offset the decreasing consumption of cigarettes by the white middle and professional classes.

In an article headlined, "Tobacco Firms, Pariahs To Many People, Still Are Angels to the Arts," the *Wall Street Journal* quotes the assistant director of development at the Whitney Museum of American Art as saying that Philip Morris is "very honorable." A Whitney Museum trustee is quoted in the same article as endorsing the company's claim to being "good citizens—not killers." And, finally, a former chairman of the board of Philip Morris adds, ". . . we are cultured human beings like anyone else, not a bunch of barbarians."[12]

The lubrication of the corporate connection to museums does not stop here. Companies now appropriate museums as sites for parties and celebratory events. Tiffany took over the Metropolitan Museum of Art for its 150th birthday anniversary, while at the same time using

the nation's foremost museum for an exhibition which amounted to
being a company history. The show was modestly titled: "Triumphs in
American Silver-Making: Tiffany & Co. 1860–1900." To conclude its
anniversary year, another of New York City's major cultural institutions, The American Museum of Natural History, was persuaded to
offer an exhibition: "Tiffany: 150 Years of Gems and Jewelry."[13] In
Boston, the Isabella Stewart Gardner Museum, never before used for
a commercial promotion, leaped into the postmodern corporate age
and turned its premises over to the Elizabeth Arden Company, which
was introducing a new perfume to city shoppers.[14]

Much as commercial television responds to its corporate sponsors'
pressure for top ratings (meaning large audiences) by organizing its
programming around star-studded, highly promoted, visually dazzling, and substantively empty shows, museums hold the blockbuster
exhibit, developed as a guaranteed means of luring huge crowds and
exposing the visiting throngs to the banners and logos of the show's
corporate sponsors. The exhibits offered, however spectacular, generally are nonprovocative and certainly unquestioning of corporate
political economy. "Most corporate sponsors finance exhibitions
based on centrist ideals and uncontroversial subject matter," one
curator reports. Thus, "sponsorship of art exhibitions helps to conceal . . . the conflict between . . . humanitarian pretenses and the
neo-imperialist expansion of multinational capitalism today by providing both the museum and the corporation with a tool for enriching individual lives while suppressing real cultural and political differences, for promoting art 'treasures' while masking private corporate
interests."[15]

Corporate sponsorship of museum exhibitions leads inevitably, as
does advertising-supported television, to self-censorship, with the
result that public awareness of social reality is continously diminished. ". . .shows that could promote critical awareness, present
products of consciousness dialectically and in relation to the social
world, or question relations of power," Haacke notes, "have a slim
chance of being approved . . . self-censorship is having a boom.
Without exerting any direct pressure, corporations have effectively
gained a veto in museums."[16] The editor of *October* magazine adds
further: "When museums now organize exhibitions, their plans must
generally take into account whether or not they will be attractive to
the boards of Philip Morris, or Exxon, United Technologies, or
Chase Manhattan. Needless to say, this affects the kinds of exhibitions undertaken and the kinds of art shown, for it is unthinkable

that a corporation would be willing to fund a show that does not enhance its image, even if indirectly."[17]

It is not only that the themes that might produce social awareness are likely to be excluded in the corporate-sponsored museum show. Equally damaging, what generally *is* presented is an alternate, but veiled, ideological message—one which emphasizes the social neutrality of art and its alleged universalistic essence. This is achieved mainly by mounting exhibits that are assemblages of discrete items, set in ahistorical arrays. The art object is abstracted from its social and historical contexts and becomes merely a product in itself—lovely perhaps, but without meaning or connection.

How this works is demonstrated in Debra Silverman's careful scrutiny of two art exhibits, one in a department store and the other in a museum—"China, [the People's Republic, that is] at Bloomingdale's and the Met."[18] Appropriately enough, Bloomingdale's, the flagship department store of affluent consumerism, organized the first of the two exhibits of the cultural legacy of the People's Republic in September 1980. Turning its sales floors into display centers of "timeless, aristocratic, and rare" Chinese goods. Bloomingdale's, for *commercial* reasons, packaged China as "timeless and aristocratic."

It was all bogus. Silverman writes: ". . . the dazzling artifacts from the People's Republic were not authentic vessels of ancient mysteries but rather the simulated products of a shrewd business alliance between the Bloomingdale's managers and the Communist Chinese Government."[19] The "rare" items were made by post-revolution "sweated craft labor." But this kind of hype is to be expected from a commercial vendor. The unsavory reputation once unique of the used-car salesman has become, quite justifiably, a generalized suspicion of salesmanship overall.

Yet the Bloomingdale's extravaganza was quickly followed, and *matched,* by an exhibit in December 1980 at the Metropolitan Museum of Art; "The Manchu Dragon: Costumes of China, the Ch'ing Dynasty, 1644–1912." The exhibit was organized and installed by Diana Vreeland, grande dame of high fashion and longtime editor of *Vogue.* Silverman compared the two shows:

> Yet despite the presumed difference between the consumerist (Bloomingdale's) and high cultural (Met) versions of China, the 1980 Met museum show shared the themes and selectivity of the Bloomingdale's packaging of China. The theme of the Met exhibition was the celebration of China as a timeless, aristocratic culture devoted to artistic crafts. . . . Historical specificity was entirely lacking from the exhibition

displays; the only guiding principle was the emphasis on the long reign of luxury and opulence signified by the rulers' magnificent clothes and elegant furniture.[20]

The message at Bloomingdale's and the Met was the same. Art has no social base. It is the product of timeless talent and creative genius. The social conditions present where it originates are irrelevant (in any case, did not appear in the shows). Individual aesthetic impulses may be gratified by such exhibits. Social understanding cannot possibly be expected. The visitor may go home satisfied in the belief of having been touched by culture. The museum and the store got their crowds and customers. The corporate sponsors filled their quota of visible public service. The loser—public awareness—was invisible and, therefore, by ratings criteria is of no account.

Measuring the Effects of Corporate Sponsorship

The corporate outreach to museums obviously is not intended to induce social instability in the political realm. Its objective is quite the opposite. Yet whether the crowds that now flow through museums—an estimated one billion passers-through in 1987—come out of them more depoliticized than when they entered is unknowable. It will remain so unless—a frightening prospect—"exit polls," such as those taken outside voting booths, are introduced. Even then, some fairly detailed questions would be required to elicit useful information. Actually, Hans Haacke tried this technique in some of his gallery shows, first in 1969 and then, more successfully, in 1971 and 1972. He asked visitors to fill out lengthy questionnaires, tabulating the answers and making them available while the exhibition remained in place to newcomers and returning information-suppliers.[21]

In 1970, Haacke asked visitors to a show that included his work at the Museum of Modern Art in New York City to ballot on the question: "Would the fact that Governor Rockefeller has not denounced President Nixon's Indochina policy be a reason for you not to vote for him in November?" At the end of the twelve-week exhibition, the ballot boxes had registered the following results:

Yes	25,566 (68.7%)
No	11,563 (31.3%)

This was an especially ironic poll, since the Museum of Modern Art (MOMA)—from its founding in 1929 through the time of the Haacke

survey in 1970 and up to the present time—is a Rockefeller fiefdom.*
Haacke, not unexpectedly, has not had another show at MOMA.

But the question remains: does the explosion in museum attendance in an era of heavy corporate cultural involvement suggest that
there are countertendencies at work that might be subversive of
corporate values and power? The evidence is absent. Perhaps the
exposure to creative work, however ahistorical and asocially presented, nourishes a general humanism, an inchoate sentiment of
nonbelligerency, an appreciation for the ecology of life. These are
speculations.

More readily appraised are the efforts of one artist—Haacke. In
doing so, it is useful to recall Enzensberger's explanation that the
consciousness industry needs creative individuals to provide it with its
raw material. Yet Enzensberger also noted that these individuals
have the opportunity, if they desire to take advantage of it, to contest
the consciousness industry's dominion and authority. Admittedly,
this is no mean task.

In the realm of museums, art galleries, and art work, Hans Haacke
has been doing just this. What he has been about has been nothing
less than stripping bare the consciousness industry itself and the place
of art and the museum as components in that industry. His works
over the last twenty years constitute a searching examination of the
connection of art to the system of power and money-making and of
the use of art to mask and conceal the rankest forms of exploitative
profit-making—slum landlordism in New York City, apartheid in
South Africa and its corporate supporters and beneficiaries, and the
advertiser's image and the reality behind it. As one critic put it,
Haacke discovered the secret of what material is *not* acceptable to the
consciousness industry. This is no small achievement, since practically everything that creative minds and talents produce is appro-
priable and usable to the advantage of the industry. What then did
Haacke produce/create that the industry rejected?

Haacke's sin, or achievement, as you will, rested "in asking how
money that might be diverted to art is actually made. . . . It is here,
in the prurient reversion to the sources of wealth, that we recognize

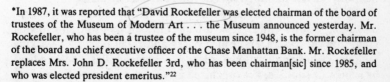

*In 1987, it was reported that "David Rockefeller was elected chairman of the board of
trustees of the Museum of Modern Art . . . the Museum announced yesterday. Mr.
Rockefeller, who has been a trustee of the museum since 1948, is the former chairman
of the board and chief executive officer of the Chase Manhattan Bank. Mr. Rockefeller
replaces Mrs. John D. Rockefeller 3rd, who has been chairman[sic] since 1985, and
who was elected president emeritus."[22]

the obscene, the unacceptable."[23] In short, Haacke's art is a schema of the political economy of art and art institutions. It is a lesson in how to critically approach the creations that customarily are brought to our attention for aesthetic edification and admiration.

Haacke, and those who do similar work in the arts, are hardly serious matches, *at this time,* for the consciousness industry. Yet they keep alive a spirit of resistance and hold the door open to alternatives, if they should appear. A heartening example of this spirit was provided by three San Diego artists, David Avalos, Louis Hock, and Elizabeth Sisco. They succeeded in eliciting a howl of indignation from the city's establishment by making a three-panelled poster, depicting the use and abuse of migrant labor in San Diego. The official outrage was deepened by the wide dissemination of the art (as placards on one hundred local transit buses) in the two weeks preceding an anticipated flood of tourists into the city to view Superbowl 1988.[24]

For all the thriving attendance at museums and art shows, the activities of the art world still represent a relatively small slice of national life—an important part to be sure and an influential one. This, in fact, is precisely why the corporate connection has been made—to build a favorable image with the affluent middle class. But beyond the museum and the gallery is the national landscape in all its breadth and variety. If the capture of the fine-arts spheres by corporate sponsorship is remarkable, the corporate presence in the American physical landscape—the city, town, and country—is astonishing.

The New Downtowns

In the postwar decades, the physical living arrangements of tens of millions of Americans changed greatly. For many reasons, most of which have had to do with profit-making from land use and transport, there occurred a massive migration of city dwellers to the suburbs.[25] This movement has been going on since the 1920s, but it accelerated dramatically after World War II. Cheap mortgages and subsidized highway construction that made the automobile the preferred mode of travel facilitated the growth of successive layers of bedroom communities outside and then well beyond the old city limits.

The continuation of this development has produced a new phenomenon, "outer cities," "an urban entity all its own: an evolving landscape of skyscrapers, office parks and retail places."[26] Lacking the familiar urban downtown, these new communities, "outer cities" or exurbs or suburbs, are organized around the automobile and provide their own site of social interaction—the shopping mall. A few malls were in existence before the war, but only after 1945 did the mall become a dominant national mode of life. By 1987, "for the first time," it is reported, "the number of shopping centers exceeded the number of post offices or secondary schools—30,600 nationwide."[27]

There is one crucial difference, however, that sets the shopping mall apart from the old, city downtown center. The mall invariably is built on privately owned real estate, which makes the *entire* mall a private domain—not only the shops, theaters, restaurants, and department stores but also the pedestrian walks, benches, and open spaces. There is no genuine public space. As one shopping-center manager explains it: "There's a general misconception that malls are public property. They are a place of public assembly, but they are private property."[28] This has its consequences. Russell Jacoby, no admirer of the new shopping centers, lamenting the disappearance of bohemias and urban intellectuals in general, still describes their features accurately:

> Malls are selling machines. Unlike city streets, they are designed and run by private companies so that every square foot, including benches and fountains, promotes a shopping mood. One corporation calls the shots, including which stores may open or stay; rents are usually based on square footage of rental space, plus a percentage of gross receipts. Obviously stores that do not yield enough do not have their leases renewed, ensuring that the mall remains homogeneous; a bookstore with too much browsing has no future. The store hours are also determined by the corporation, and since few people live close by and none live in the malls [no longer true], they are deserted after 6:00 or 9:00 P.M.[29]

John Friedmann, head of the Urban Planning Program in the Graduate School of Architecture at the University of California, Los Angeles, describes the urban equivalent of the mall—the shopping centers—which have grown up in Los Angeles in recent years:

> The first few stories of each centre are typically devoted to parking. (It costs more to build a parking space in Los Angeles than to house a working class family in Latin America, a rough estimate is $15,000 per slot). The rest is developed as a series of pedestrian malls. Shopping centres are air-conditioned mazes, given over to the single activity of spending money. As you stroll from window to window, piped music relaxing any vestigial buyer-resistance you may still offer, TV monitors discreetly observe your every move, their unblinking eyes rotating indefatigably in 120 degree arcs. And the ever-present Pinkerton guards in

their blue uniforms can be seen to murmur secrets in their walkie-talkies, reporting to Central Control, ever watchful of the slightest irregularity in this environment, controlled to perfection, this fascist Utopia.[30]

The pervasive commercialization of malls makes them, in Jacoby's view and in actuality, inhospitable places for restless intellectuals and social nonconformists. But there is a still more grievous impact that affects the entire community and which, because it is part of the institutional structure of the mall, surfaces only infrequently. The private ownership of the shopping center—its primary characteristic—makes it also an inhospitable place for the free circulation of ideas, to say nothing of social action. It is a locale where the likelihood of independent thinking, let alone action, is matter-of-factly excluded.

Just how much jurisdiction and ultimate control can be exercised by the mall's key private owner, often the main department store in the complex, is by no means a settled matter across the country. The legal approval of full, private-ownership control of the mall varies from state to state, though in recent years, reflecting the national expansion of corporate influence, the right of shopping-center owners increasingly has been given precedence over other claims. Some states allow, for example, distributing political and social pamphlets in malls. Others permit the mall's owners to exclude such activities.

A New York State Court of Appeals ruling in December 1985 is indicative of recent court thinking. In that decision, the court ruled that the owner of a private shopping mall had the legal right to enforce a blanket no-handbill policy. Also, he did not have to permit leaflet distribution—in this particular case, leaflets opposing nuclear energy. The ruling of the court was instructive in its interpretation of what kind of protection the state constitution's Bill of Rights conferred on the citizenry. In its view, the constitution ". . . governed the rights of citizens with respect to their government and not the rights of private individuals against private individuals." In sum, the citizen of New York State is protected against state actions that violate individual rights but defenseless against violations that may originate in the private sector, imposed by private-property owners.

To the extent that private-property owners legally can decide what kind of activity is permissible in their malls, a vast and still expanding terrain is withdrawn from serving as a site of public expression. Yet more than the subtraction of a large chunk of real estate from public use is involved here. It is heavily used space which now largely constitutes the main public thoroughfares of the nation. The dissenting opinion of the chief justice of the New York State Court of Appeals emphasized this point in particular:

> The conclusion, (reached by the lower courts) that the mall has all the attributes of a downtown business area or town center is inescapable. It is also evident, in light of the large number of people who congregate at the mall, the exercise of free speech by those who seek to communicate with the general public will be adversely affected by a complete denial of access to the mall.

The judge concluded:

> . . . In the past, those who had ideas they wished to communicate to the public had the unquestioned right to disseminate those ideas in the open marketplace. Now that the marketplace has a roof over it, and is called a mall, we should not abridge that right.[31]

In any case, across the country in more than 30,000 shopping centers, a great variety of personal and commercial activities involve millions of people in daily interactions. For the most part, and increasingly, political expression and social action are not included. The mall, whether or not originally intended to provide a substitute for urban downtowns, has become the ideal landscape for corporate America. It brings masses of people together to buy goods and services and, by virtue of its peculiar feudal patterns of ownership (with some few shining exceptions), effectively insulates them from seeing, hearing, or encountering expression and ideas that might, however slightly, disturb the mood, routines, and tranquillity of daily shopping. The mall comes as close as can be managed to a total corporate-commercial environment. Distilled out are all the conflicts seeking solutions. What are left are fast-food preparations and movies which also are likely to be cleansed of divisive content.

The Old Downtowns and City Public Spaces

While suburban development boomed and shopping malls proliferated, the cities from which the new suburbanites fled were undergoing their own transformations. During the early postwar years, making up for the heavy outmigration of young and upwardly mobile whites, many city centers were repopulated with the left-behind poor, the new poor, and waves of black migrants dispossessed by the mechanized agriculture in the South. A more recent, second wave of change, still underway, is the ousting of the city-center poor by a stream of returning, relatively affluent, professional young people.

The effects of the stock-market collapse in the fall of 1987 and of possible future economic debacles on this new influx are still to be seen. For the moment, at least, the condominium, boutique, expensive restaurant scene continues to flourish in the downtowns of many American cities. The urban poor are removed to the city's fringes, while the most helpless and desperate roam the streets and huddle in darkened doorways.

In the city center, the developers are the new urban princes. Corporate-headquarters buildings and commercial office towers crowd out people in downtown areas. Developers and their architects, sometimes to mollify the community troubled by the destruction of public space, include small concrete parks and "gardens" in their sky-high atriums or at the street level of their gigantic edifices.* Here, city walkers may sit, often uncomfortably in steel-mesh (so they will not be vandalized) chairs. They may be surrounded by some imported palms and ferns, behind or alongside of which are the never-absent luxury shops, trying to prosper despite their own excessive rents. Architectural critic Ada Louise Huxtable assessed the recent surge of building in New York—the Empire City, banking and information hub of the transnational corporate world:

> What is new and notable in New York City's unprecedented building boom is that all previous legal, moral and aesthetic restraints have been thrown to the winds, or more accurately, to the developers . . .

---

*Two highly publicized and visible examples are the "public plazas," that were built as part of the IBM and AT&T huge corporate-headquarters buildings on New York City's Madison Avenue in the midtown area. The *New York Times* architecture columnist, Paul Goldberger, described the deal that produced these public benefits: ". . . these two were constructed as a result of a zoning trade-off; if builders agreed to include these public amenities, they were permitted to make their buildings 20 percent larger than the zoning laws would otherwise allow." After describing this "trade-off," Goldberger comes to an astonishing conclusion: "So these plazas are not really a gift to the people from the buildings' owners—they are much more a gift from the city itself."[32] More accurately, the only "gift" readily evident in the transaction was the permission given to the builders to violate the zoning codes by 20 percent. The public got a couple of dubious resting places, surrounded by masonry. A genuine choice might have meant an undeveloped street corner with a real park instead of IBM's and AT&T's massive presence. A plaque, prominently displayed in the AT&T "plaza" aptly describes the current condition of authority: It reads:
PUBLIC SPACE
Owned and Maintained
by A.T.& T.
550 Madison Ave., N.Y.C.

The reorientation of priorities has created a climate in which zoning controls, developed and tested over 70 years no longer have credibility or support; their exploitation is active policy. The city is wide open. Greed has never been so chic. The public interest has never been so passé.[33]

The same disregard is observable in cities across the nation—in city or shopping mall, public space is the victim. In the suburbs, genuine public space in the malls does not exist. In the city downtowns, gigantic structures, built disregarding every notion of human scale, crowd out the possibility of public street life.

Still, there are other interpretations of these urban-suburban developments. One generous view opines that

A sure way of finding the kinds of public spaces from which people gain pleasure is to see where they most like to go. The "atriums" of some new Manhattan skyscrapers (often built partly in response to the pressures of city planners) are places that people seem to find interesting, both in themselves and for the opportunities they provide to be with other people. It is contrary to observation to think that people usually seek to avoid crowds. One attraction of the shopping mall—however functional and one-dimensional its purpose and however excessive the role of shopping in capitalist societies—is that it provides a sense of place, as well as a convenient solution to the problem of parking a car. The places tourists like to go are another index, tourists being ourselves as well as other people.[34]

The assumption in this accommodating account of the current urban-suburban spatial scene is that people actually have a choice of where they go when they come to a downtown skyscraper's concrete "plaza." But where else can they find a spot to rest their aching feet?

The Control of the Street

The use of public streets in the city has been a "site" of social struggle as far back as the early nineteenth century—to say nothing of earlier strife in European centers. The propertied and well-to-do classes always have feared large numbers of people in the streets, especially if the streets were in their neighborhood and, even more so, if the people were assembling to express political and economic grievances.

Folklorist Susan Davis surveyed the parade in Philadelphia in the 1800s. She reviewed the efforts that were made by those concerned with law and order and the preservation of private property to pacify and regularize the people's use of the streets for demonstrations and marches. Comparing the current scene with the earlier, nineteenth-century, popular though contested uses of the city's space, she concludes:

> Nineteenth-century constraints and limitations on public uses of the street have thus been strengthened and dramatically extended. The collective uses of the streets and open spaces are now determined almost entirely by the interests of private enterprise. . . . Because of the combined forces of commerce and the demand for order, open spaces have become much less lively milieux. Parades, as we know them today, give only a carefully prefabricated appearance of ties to a genuine community life.[35]

Similarly, John Friedmann, urban planning theorist, believes that "a city can truly be called a city only when its streets belong to the people." He notes further that there are "only two occasions when people take to the street and claim it as their own: when they arise in protest against the authority of an oppressive state, and when they celebrate."[36] In postwar America, the people have not taken to the streets to protest against an oppressive state, though there have been major demonstrations in support of civil rights—to protest the war in Vietnam and to seek international peace. Public celebrations are another matter.

Since the development of television and its widespread penetration of American homes in the late 1940s and early 1950s, there has been a galloping commercialization of public celebrations, demonstrations, and parades. Longtime popular festivals and fetes are appropriated by corporate sponsors, and in the process, the meaning and history of the event is lost or transformed into a vacuous show. The creation of new and often bogus celebrations is a thriving business. The more an event can be presented as a spectacle, suitable for television viewing and corporate sponsorship, the greater the likelihood of its appropriation.

The well-known, commercial-TV producer of the national celebration of Independence Day and the centennial of the Statue of Liberty (a four-day "show") was uncomprehending that a federal judge would refuse to participate in his scenario of a nationwide naturalization ceremony because advertising would accompany the televised program. A spokesperson for the producer complained: "You could have had these people on the steps of the Jefferson Memorial. It could have been seen by a billion and a half people around the world. I just don't understand these people, the judges."[37]

This judge's unwillingness to be part of a political propaganda-commercial extravaganza was exceptional. Rarely is there reluctance from any quarter to miss an opportunity for exploiting a public event for profit. In this case, the naturalization ceremony, as part of Liberty Weekend, was "conceived with television in mind, and rights to cover key portions of it were sold exclusively to ABC-TV for $10 million."[38]

To insure that the two-hundredth anniversary of the Constitution, beginning in the fall of 1987, would be a properly acknowledged event, the chief justice of the Supreme Court relinquished his judicial position and "has been trying to mobilize the resources of America's large corporations for a big party in honor of the document."[39] Chief Justice Berger traded his Supreme Court seat for a fund-raising assignment.

The seizure of public events and celebrations for corporate commercial advantage strikes a double blow at the public's interest and well-being. It allows still another part of public life and history to be turned into a sales promotion—as if there were insufficient opportunity for commercial solicitation in the daily routines of American life. More damaging still, authentic historical experiences and the community's memory are emptied of meaning in the corporate-managed festivals. In their place are the frictionless social events, synthetic, up-beat concoctions that life insurance companies, banks, and department stores feel comfortable with. One can look in vain for the social struggles that mark American life and history in the sanitized commercial pageants that now regularly fill TV screens and national landscapes.

Party life also, at the upper social levels in the nation's capital, has become a corporate enterprise. One events-planning executive of a company engaged in catering shared this account: "Every day, every night, there must be hundreds of corporate-sponsored events taking place, from launching a perfume to a party for 2,000 on the Mall. . . . Another caterer which averages 10,000 parties a year, reports that 80 percent of its business is now corporate-driven."[40]

For less-affluent folk, unable to afford or not invited to such elaborate party-going, block and city-street celebrations have become frequent events. These provide enjoyment and sociability. Yet here as well, despite the efforts and enthusiasm of local participants, banners across the avenues proclaim the goodwill and endorsement of the local, though major, banks or whatever corporations deem it useful to be associated with such local activities.

Indeed, wherever people congregate, the corporate presence is manifest and heavily publicized. The month of June (1988) was a particularly busy time. The Chemical Bank advertised its sponsorship of opera in New York's Central Park.[41] AT&T was "On Stage," supporting plays at a New York Summer Festival.[42] Shearson Lehman Hutton, the securities firm, "presented Bill Cosby in Concert."[43] Philip Morris, the cigarette company, in a two-page, color spread in the *New York Times Magazine,* headlined the appearance of Harlem's Dance Theatre in New York City.[44]

These are rewarding events. People benefit from what seems to be a social subsidy provided by the corporate sector. But there is a cost too! The public's attention is focused on the corporation as social benefactor. Its actual dominant role as resource allocator for private interests is thereby more likely to escape the scrutiny it deserves.

Public Television Space

Much of the nation's physical space, outdoors and indoors, is now a private preserve, carrying the messages and culture of the corporations that dominate economic and political life. Their domain also extends to another kind of space—the airwaves. These provide access to the most personal places of daily life; the living room, the bedroom, and the kitchen.

Television (though much of academe still regards it as unworthy of scholarly attention) is now one of the most influential, largely unacknowledged educators in the country. One reason why television is heavily discounted as a powerful educational force is the distinction made between "educational" and "entertainment" programming. This artificial separation seems to mesmerize many into believing that entertainment shows are not educational.

Only big business has the money and the confidence to challenge—when its own interest is adversely affected—the accepted notion that entertainment is "value-free." The chairman of a major transnational corporation, J. Peter Grace, was outraged when the three national commercial-television networks rejected a commercial his company wanted to run about the federal deficit. Their reason was that they considered the deficit a controversial issue of public importance that should be taken up by the news division. Grace and his legal counsel, Joseph A. Califano, wrote a tough op-ed piece for the *New York Times:*

> . . . the networks can't be serious when they argue that only news divisions and their people should deal with matters of public controversy.

They should spend some time glancing at the programs broadcast by their entertainment divisions. There is hardly a public issue affecting American life that is not in some way touched upon by these programs: abortion, the right to life, nuclear holocaust, homosexuality, drug addiction, racial discrimination, crime, the activities of the intelligence agencies. Is there really any doubt that controversial issues are an integral part of the totality of television—and that their "coverage" goes way beyond their news programs? Moreover, who can tell where news divisions end and entertainment divisions begin?[45]

Grace and Califano may have overstated the amount of controversial material on commercial television, but they are on target in calling attention to the value-laden character of so-called entertainment programming.

Recognized as educational or not, the influence of omnipresent television (based on the amount of time consumed in viewing) far surpasses that of total formal education. Today, for a large part of the population, TV is the teacher, though the lessons transmitted rarely are recognized as such. Some do see this, however. Benjamin Barber, examining the currently fashionable view that American youngsters are "cultural morons" and need a good dose of "basic" education, writes:

They [the kids] are society-smart rather than school-smart. They are adept readers—but not of books. What they read so acutely are the social signals that emanate from the world in which they will have to make a living. Their teachers in this world—the nation's true pedagogues—are television, advertising, movies, politics and the celebrity domains they define.[46]

Since its arrival in the late 1940s, television has served essentially as a marketing instrument, flooding viewers with thousands of advertisements, dozens of them inserted in each transmitted hour. In 1985, on network (national) television alone (excluding local-station advertising), there were 5,131 commercials broadcast weekly.[47]

The near-total utilization of television for corporate marketing represents at the same time the daily ideological instruction of the viewing audience. This occurs, first of all, in the incessant identification of consumerism with democracy. Marketing has become so much a part of the political process that it is increasingly difficult to determine where it leaves off and politics begins.

In the early presidential campaigning in the fall of 1987, for example, twelve candidates (six Democrats and six Republicans) engaged in a televised debate. Naturally, it was sponsored. NBC News could not be expected to provide a "free" hour for such a purpose. The sponsors were the Ford Motor Company, The Travelers Corporation, and Wang Laboratories, Inc. Each of these companies received approximately the same amount of time for their commercials as each candidate was allowed to offer his program. A viewer could be excused for believing the commercials were part of the debate and that perhaps each company had its own presidential candidate.[48]

But most important of all, the programming that is sandwiched between the commercials invariably is produced by the cultural industry to satisfy, or at least not upset, the sponsor. The consequence is that rarely is a program of serious social criticism broadcast. The airwaves overflow with *personal* crises and conflicts. The major divisions that characterize American society are glaringly absent.

One development in American broadcasting that has special saliency for the rest of the world, to say nothing of the domestic social well-being, is the fate of public (noncommercial) television. Never a strong institution (as it has been in Western Europe and elsewhere), public broadcasting has lost most of the little autonomous space it once briefly held. Always short of resources and given the less preferred part of the frequency spectrum—the UHF band—public broadcasting did succeed, on the basis of some program importation and some thoughtful domestic cultural material, to gain a small though affluent and influential slice of the national viewing audience in the 1970s and '80s.

These high-income viewers who were attracted to the noncommercial channels (though hardly a mass audience) constituted an important opinion-making group and a high-disposable-income class. It was inevitable that they would become a target of the big, luxury-goods advertisers. At first, discreet announcements at the beginning and the end of the programs indicated that the shows were being made available by courtesy of some public-spirited corporation. Once the corporate foot was in the door, the erosion of the noncommercial broadcast principle accelerated. Under what it called "enhanced guidelines" (a soothing euphemism to conceal the destruction intended), the deregulation-obsessed Federal Communications Commission (FCC) in 1984 allowed greater scope for sponsors' messages. A year later, the country's foremost newspaper, apparently uneasy with the reality but reluctant to confront it directly, was inquiring editorially: "Is Public TV Becoming Overly Commercial?"[49]

In the fall of 1987, the FCC for the umteenth time launched an inquiry into children's television, the commercialization of which has been a national scandal for decades. In an agency statement reeking with hypocrisy, it was reported that "The FCC said it will try to determine whether the marketplace has 'failed' children, whether it was appropriate for the government to regulate these failures, and whether such regulation would violate the First Amendment."[50]

The cultural industry offers its own "solution" to the wasteland that is children's TV. Home Box Office (HBO), Time, Inc.'s pay channel, informs parents that it is in *their* (the parents') *hands* "to determine what your children watch." HBO proceeds to selectively endorse some of the suggestions of the liberal, nonprofit organization, Action for Children's Television (ACT). Not surprisingly, they fit nicely with HBO's program offerings. ACT recommends that the viewing hours of children be regulated and that they "watch *specific* programs, not just watch television." HBO has the added presumption to state: "We help by offering commercial-free family programming."[51]

The pervasive commercialization of television is a direct outcome of the cultural industry's appropriation of the medium of television for marketing. Now, one of the most powerful of the cultural/media conglomerates, Time, Inc., offers to provide, *at a price,* programming which is not interlarded with commercials. HBO's offer is breathtaking. It is the equivalent of a papermill company first polluting a town's water supply and then congratulating itself for offering to provide the community, for a price, with purified water.

Still, popular dissatisfaction with children's programming is strong, and Congress is compelled to pay attention and offer some support to those seeking to reduce the sales pitches to the kiddies. Legislative efforts to limit commercials in children's TV were initiated in 1988.[52] In keeping with eight years of promoting deregulation and as one of his last acts in office, President Reagan vetoed a congressional bill (in November 1988) that would have placed extremely modest ceilings on TV commercials aired during children's programming.[53] How far these efforts will proceed and how much they will change current patterns will be decided by the strength of the contending forces, numerous but unorganized consumer and parent groups and highly concentrated and powerfully organized broadcasting interests.

From time to time, also, proposals circulate to finance an expanded, noncommercial television system by taxes on, for example, the resale of stations/channels or on receiver equipment. An effort along these lines advanced to the final stages of congressional action in the winter of 1987. At the last moment, the proposal to levy such a tax was deleted from the bill. The chair of the senate committee proposing the measure, Senator Ernest F. Hollings, acknowledged that the media owners are more powerful than Congress: "We had unanimity," he said, "but the broadcasters are way more powerful."[54]

American public television has never been a flourishing enterprise. Its long-term debility is mostly symptomatic of a more general national malaise—the seizure of most of the country's cultural space by corporate business. Yet fleeing from the corporate colonization of consciousness is less and less realistic. Beyond the national frontiers the same conditions are present. The transnational corporate system and its cultural infrastructure are global phenomena. How this affects the international information-cultural environment is the concern of the next chapter.

| 6 |

The Transnationalization of Corporate Expression

The phenomenal growth of American capitalism in the years after 1945 helps to explain the deep penetration of corporate values and influence in American politics, law, education, culture, and life overall. Yet this influence has by no means been confined to continental boundaries. A good part of the corporate growth is accounted for by the transnational operations and undertakings of major companies in the early postwar years. These were mostly American-owned. More recently, European, Japanese, and big companies from other lands have become active also.

To be sure, overseas investment and manufacturing operations abroad existed long before World War II. Also, in the early postwar years, the U.S. media combines actively cultivated and penetrated the international market. More recent developments, however, are qualitatively different. The new information technologies that have been introduced have created a substantially changed international economic order. In the new world economy, national states, including the most powerful, are subjected to the imperatives, practices, and flows of transnational capital. The moves of the big players in the international arena, the transnational corporations, have become profoundly consequential, if not determining.

Predictably, it was in the United States that the initial and decisive patterns were worked out. These facilitated corporate domination domestically over the social, political, and economic realms. Soon thereafter, this authority was extended into the international sphere.

That the United States should have been the initiating site of these far-reaching changes was a natural consequence of the privileged condition of American capitalism at the end of World War II. Benefitting from the war itself and enjoying several years of uncontested global market supremacy in the years immediately thereafter, the expansion of capital and the rapid growth in the assets of American companies were unmatched. Naturally, this unprecedented accumulation of corporate wealth and economic power would press its advantage in all directions. And it did! All the same, a modest share of this vast revenue flow was passed along to the domestic work force, at least its organized portion. Additionally, some of the mildly redistributive social programs that had been established in the depression years of the 1930s were maintained and even slightly expanded.

This seemingly generous behavior of American corporate leadership gave rise to a certain amount of illusion about the allegedly changed nature of capitalism. Most of it was dispelled with the return of international competition which began to cut into U.S. markets and profits in the late 1960s and early 1970s.

Of the many moves by which American industry strove to improve, or at least maintain, its position domestically and worldwide, the most important, with the most far-reaching consequences, was the policy of deregulation. This strategy received strong government support as well beginning in the mid-1970s. Its fullest implementation occurred during the Reagan years.

Deregulation, wherever it was applied, was intended to reduce or eliminate entirely public scrutiny and oversight of business activity— i.e., pricing, profit levels, safety, labor policy, consumer protection, environmental monitoring, foreign trade, and intra-industry coordination. One recent study of the deregulatory wave in the United States began with a question: "Is deregulation . . . a strategy on the part of capital to reappropriate the power it once lost to democratic reforms [of the '30s and mid-'60s?]"[1]

It is indeed! It is also a strategy to overcome the heavy competitive pressure of the international market by weakening labor and its political influence. In doing so, the corporate wage bill and other social costs are expected to be reduced. It is a perfectly rational calculation, supported by a century and a half of capitalist history and experience. This can be regarded as the *defensive* side of deregulation. It is intended to make the U.S. economy more efficient. Not unimportant, a second outcome is the maintenance of profits at levels high enough to satisfy investors and lure new suppliers of capital.

Deregulation has its *offensive* side as well. It removes, in some instances, the restraints and prohibitions on companies. It allows them to ally with others, disregarding antitrust and other restrictions. It permits them to enter fully into international markets and operations. In the field of telecommunications, this has had an impact extending far beyond an admittedly important sector in its own right. It has accelerated the concentration of communication power in the United States. It has forced changes, some of which are still underway, in Europe and other parts of the world that are contributing to a restructuring of the international economy.

The ease with which information and capital circulate globally, due in large measure to the new information technologies, is changing the international division of labor and shifting production sites across the world. One example of this is the worldwide infrastructure of Texas Instruments, Inc. (TI). "Texas Instruments, Inc. relies on a global network of 37 mainframe computers and 41,500 work-stations on five continents." "The $300 million-plus system," *Business Week* reports, "routes 160,000 electronic mail messages and 127,000 file transfers daily."[2]

In tracing the main lines and identifying the key players in the deregulation of American communications, one point needs special emphasis. What began as a domestic restructuring for internal economic reasons has had a global impact. This has led some to view the examination and analysis of the forces that have contributed to a worldwide realignment of economic activity and power as an exercise in what they like to call "conspiracy theory." Intentionality and a hidden game plan are the features of such an outlook.

The idea and the charge are both absurd. Telecommunications deregulation in the United States has been a long and complicated process. Massive litigation, shifting positions of the litigants, and accommodation and compromise are involved. Some of the decisions which have been made are still surrounded with ambiguity. To explain this tortuous and complex process as a simple-minded scheme to run the world would be ludicrous.

At the same time, it would be naive to believe that the major economic actors engaged in the development and deployment of telecommunications networks and computers are unaware of the stakes in the game. It has been evident, since the earliest moves, that communication was destined to be a, if not *the,* dominant industry in the twenty-first century. In pursuing their own ends, the transnational corporations produced a dynamic that became the motor force influencing economic and cultural developments far from home and far into the future.

In the United States, much of the communication deregulatory process revolved around the movement to break up ("divest") AT&T, the de facto American telecommunications monopoly. AT&T was not just another big corporation. It was the single largest private enterprise in the country. Its lobby dominated Congress for decades. Its influence was felt in the smallest town. Yet in 1982, an agreement was reached which divested AT&T of its operating companies. It allowed the corporation to keep its core activities—research laboratories, manufacturing units, long-lines communications—and, most important, allowed it for the first time to enter the international market of telecommunications and computers. This was a freedom heretofore denied the company.

How to account for this successful effort to curtail unrivaled corporate power, which up to that time was practically unchallengeable? AT&T was "mugged" by its *corporate-user* clientele—especially the biggest companies who were the heaviest communication users. Their communication costs had become major operational expenditures. Accordingly, the big corporate users of AT&T's facilities and services wanted to reduce their communication costs and, also, to have the freedom to apply the new information technologies to their specific operational requirements. Fortuitously for these users, the appearance of new and flexible information technologies in the preceding decades—microwave transmission, computerization, satellite communication—made feasible for the first time an alternative to total reliance on the domestic private monopoly. They also promised to reduce considerably the communications bills of these companies.

Finally, the expanded scale of operations to the international arena, totally reliant on communications, encouraged a few hundred major U.S. companies to press for the breakup of AT&T. In doing so, they anticipated a free field to make whatever communication arrangements suited them best.[3] They pursued their quest through all the channels available to them—the courts, Congress, the regulatory agencies, and even the media.

The AT&T decision was a foretaste of the experience of *national* telecommunications systems in Europe and elsewhere. The means by which the dominant U.S. companies got their way against one of their own, and the mightiest one at that, are being replicated in one country after another—with one essential difference. The power and influence of giant, private corporations, directed toward obtaining information capabilities at the lowest possible costs, in much of the rest of the world go up against *nationally run* communication entities, broadcasting systems, and posts and telegraph and telephone administrations (PTTs). AT&T is a *private* enterprise, but the underlying significance of the AT&T divestiture decision (and of deregulation overall in the communication sector) is that it opened the way to the destruction of national oversight in the information field, probably the most important sector of economic and cultural life in the years ahead.

Another Pressure Point Against
National Communication Oversight

Acknowledging the motives and strength of the corporate-driven deregulation dynamic in the communication sector is not to deny or exclude the presence of other factors as well. The most important of these additional forces has been the U.S. government, acting on behalf of its corporate constituency. The federal government has served as a powerful agent in promoting privatization and deregulation throughout the world. One persuasive account suggests that the vehement hostility of the Reagan administration to the United Nations system in general, and to the United Nations Educational, Scientific, and Cultural Organization (UNESCO) in particular, can best be understood as an effort to destroy the international public sector.[4] In doing so, it eliminates the alternative to transnational corporate enterprise.

By weakening UNESCO, for example, the capability of an international organization to defend the informational interests of its members against transnational corporate activity is undermined. Colleen Roach, a former U.S. employee of UNESCO, observes that the main argument used by U.S. officials to attack UNESCO is "its supposed intent of promoting government-controlled media." It hardly matters whether this was a justified accusation. The main motive of the attack on UNESCO has been the desire to weaken public-sector communications structures which have long existed in many nations. Roach writes: "The imperative for U.S. transnational telecommunications business interests is concretely reflected in the 'deregulatory fever' and the move toward the privatization of the public sector. This coupling of the deregulatory and privatization movements necessarily undermines a strong public sector of the economy whether on a national or international basis."[5]

The unilateral withdrawal of the United States from UNESCO in 1984, in this perspective, can be seen as the American government's encouragement of deregulation and privatization in the international arena and in the poorer countries especially.

It is in the poor part of the world that U.S. government intervention is most intense and least ambiguous. It usually is indirectly applied but, nonetheless, effective. It is managed mostly by denying, in principle and practice, economic assistance to impoverished countries unless they abandon their public-sector national enterprises and undertakings. These policies of denial operate against international agencies which function on some minimal standard of majority decision-making and full participation of their members. Never thoroughly acceptable as a mechanism to American leadership from the earliest postwar years, the U.S. government has become less and less inclined to contribute funds for economic or social assistance through the United Nations and its related organizations.

In the Reagan era, the shut-off of funds to such organizations has been tightened. At the 1987 United Nations Conference on Trade and Development (UNCTAD), for example, where trade and development issues were discussed and Third World needs presented, the Reagan administration sent a low-ranking representative to a conference which was largely at the ministerial and sub-ministerial level. "It's intended to show contempt." one U.S. official commented. The official delegate described himself as "the traveling insult."[6]

At still another major conference convened by the United Nations to consider the possibility and feasibility of transferring funds to the developmental needs of the poor world *if* disarmament actually occurred, the United States alone of all the Western industrialized nations refused to attend. Its official position was that disarmament and development were two separate, unrelated matters.[7]

While withholding money from multilateral programs administered by international organizations functioning on a one-nation, one-vote rule, the United States imposes its deregulatory and privatization criteria on the lending policies of the banks and developmental bodies to which it is the largest contributor and in which it exercises a de-facto veto. Countries which seek to borrow from the World Bank, various development banks and the International Monetary Fund, for example, find that loans are contingent on their relinquishing national control of industry. They are pressured into adopting policies that encourage private capital investment and private ownership. Enterprises that are administered by national authority are denationalized and put up for sale.

In the late 1980s, the global offensive of transnational capital, assisted by U.S. government pressure, is striking. The *New York Times,* for example, reports "The Global March to Free Markets."[8] In Africa, "a rush to privatize" is discovered and ten "privatizing" states are listed. Another report announces that an "African Enclave Forsakes Marxism."[9] This surge to free enterprise is attributed to failures of nationalization and the accompanying disillusionment of these countries' leaders. Perhaps this is so. Also possible is the rigid denial of capital from the main foreign suppliers in Western Europe, the United States, and Japan unless privatization is adopted. An example of how this is effected is the following report on the withholding and then resumption of aid to Ethiopia:

> The World Bank and several Western nations will resume agricultural aid to Ethiopia, which has agreed to create new incentives for food production to combat a famine, United Nations officials and diplomats say.
>
> The policy change by Ethiopia's Marxist Government is seen as an important success for the West's position of linking new development aid for the poorest African countries to market-oriented policies that encourage farmers and businesses to increase production.
>
> The World Bank suspended new assistance for rural farmers in 1984. The European Community signed a five-year $250 million aid program with Ethiopia in 1985, but it has refused to allocate the money for rural agricultural development since then.[10]

In the communication sector, the privatization pressure is especially intense. How to pay for the expensive programming of indigenous production and for up-to-date equipment? In noncommercial systems, viewer charges are high and relatively inflexible, though costs continue to increase. (It is politically difficult to increase frequently the license tax that pays for television or radio service). These circumstances affect the developed market economies no less than the poor, newly independent nations. In the latter, the situation is culturally disastrous.

There is another, and not inconsequential, factor in the recent successes of capital in penetrating and weakening national information-communication institutions and national enterprise in general. In Europe, especially, it is the long-standing failure of national broadcasting and telecommunications entities to achieve genuine popular support. Why this has been so differs from country to country and from industry to industry. Still, there are some common features that have marked the operation and behavior of state-administered communication enterprises.

A particularly instructive example is the British Broadcasting Corporation (BBC). This institution seems to have more admirers outside of than inside of the country. Paternalistic, elitest, stodgy, and status-quo oriented are some of the less hostile descriptions of the BBC by its domestic critics. This lack of enthusiasm for the national broadcasting system, especially by those who it might be thought would be its strongest defenders, contributes significantly to the success of the commercializing and privatizing forces. The state structures are left without support or, at best, tepid endorsement, while their corporate envelopment moves forward relentlessly.

However justified the criticisms of the state broadcasting and informational organizations may be, their dismantlement and replacement by market-driven systems leads inevitably, perhaps irreversibly, to the full-scale triumph of transnational culture. The next section examines briefly how this works.

The Deregulation Dynamic

The corporate deregulatory dynamic in the cultural-informational field proceeds along two paths. First, it seeks to promote and protect the *general* commercial-information activities of the transnational corporate system and its major players. The second aim is to satisfy the specific marketing needs of those corporations who are engaged in consumer-goods-and-services production and whose sales require heavy and continued access to national media systems. Alongside these overarching aims are the not inconsiderable interests of large transnational media companies to operate globally without restrictions.

For these objectives to be realized, national control over the informational system is seen to be an obstacle which must be removed or, at least, greatly reduced. This, in fact, is the task assigned to deregulation—or "liberalization" as it is termed in Western Europe.

Transnational Corporate Information Needs

At the general systemic level, deregulation translates into the abrogation of national sovereignty. The case for disposing of that irksome condition is made forthrightly by the Business Roundtable. The Roundtable is a domestic grouping that includes the chief executives of the few hundred most powerful corporations in America. The Roundtable sets out its rationale by first explaining the importance of information flows to transnational business:

In the past fifteen years, the flow of information across national borders has increased dramatically. This international information flow (IIF) includes everything from internal corporate information transfers to trade in information-based products and services. IIF has expanded international markets and made possible the provision of new products and services to those markets. IIF has allowed multinational enterprises to improve their services to their customers, consolidate their resources, control their costs, and reduce their financial risks. IIF has transformed the way in which all companies, manufacturing or service, do business internationally.[11]

The Roundtable puts at the top of its information-policy-issues agenda the free flow of information—*its* information. It states: "The free flow of information internationally advances the human condition and enhances both national economies and the world economy." Accordingly, "The U.S. approaches [all information questions] from the premise that the 'free flow of information' should be foremost, and that any exceptions to this principle for other over-riding public policy interests should be limited and narrowly drawn."[12] The Roundtable, understandably, defines the "free flow of information" in a way which corresponds fully with transnational corporate information needs and imperatives. Not inconsequentially, this definition fuses economic, political, and cultural ends.

It follows that given the vital importance of unrestricted commercial and business information flows to the transnational corporate order, national control or oversight of any kind of these flows is deemed intolerable. The Roundtable, the U.S. government, and the U.S. media are in full agreement on this matter. If the Roundtable and its allies had their way, the entire informational-cultural sector would be withdrawn from national responsibility. It makes no secret of this sentiment:

> The sovereign right of nations to determine their own telecommunications policies is not the issue; rather it is the international consequences of these national policies that may be subject to legitimate challenge by other countries whose interests are adversely affected.[13]

In this corporate perspective, it is not the transgressor of national sovereignty who is at fault. Indeed, defense against that aggression is cited as a violation of international norms. In other words, the exercise of national sovereignty in the corporate view is incompatible with the "free flow of information." Since free flow is the cardinal principle of transnational capital—whether it be applied to information, capital, or labor—it is national sovereignty that must be abandoned. George Ball, former under secretary of state in the Kennedy and Johnson administrations, and one of the more farsighted defenders of the transnational corporate order, put the national sovereignty issue this way:

> On the economic side, we have to take account of the fact that our political structure is totally inadequate for a world where technology has assured that capital flows move around without regard to national boundaries. Sooner or later, we're going to have to face restructuring our institutions so that they're not confined merely to the nation states.[14]

The restructuring that Ball foresees and is recommending has, up to now at least, been made the responsibility of *other* nations. One of the sticking points in the protracted U.S.–Canadian negotiations for establishing a comprehensive, free-trade pact between the two countries is Canada's concern to safeguard its cultural industries against the "free flow of information." A rancorous election on the issue in November 1988 gave the free traders a parliamentary majority but "failed to persuade a majority of voters that the free-trade agreement did not threaten Canadian sovereignty and the Canadian way of life."[15]

The Marketing Dynamic

Once the principle that transnational corporate information flows are inviolable is established, the deregulation dynamic moves inexorably to cut further into the national social fabric. Not only must corporate information flows be allowed international circulation, they must also be granted full access to national media channels. Anything less, claim the transnationals—with the authority of the U.S. government supporting them—is to deny freedom, the freedom of corporate speech. This claim must be understood as more than rhetorical flourish or an idiosyncratic appeal to democratic ritual. It represents rather the deepest systemic requirements of contemporary capitalism.

It is inherent in the present-day international economy that a transnational company establishes subsidiaries and branches in many national locales in the expectation of selling its goods and services to the host population, as well as exporting the product wherever it can. Still, an automatic willingness of local populations to purchase and consume these outputs cannot be taken for granted. The mechanisms of consumer persuasion and titillation—carried to their highest efficiency in the United States—are relied on. They are applied, sometimes with modification, to take into account national cultural specificities. The objective, whatever the national setting, is always the same—the creation of good consumers.

Still there are problems. Until recently, national broadcasting systems in many parts of the world were reluctant to open their circuits unreservedly to corporate speech, advertising in particular. To the degree that a national system has shown recalcitrance to the advertising demands of transnational capital, it has moved into the area targeted by the transnationals for deregulation. Similarly, if a national telecommunications system (PTT) has resisted the demands of the big corporate communication users for greater corporate communications autonomy, the national system also encounters the deregulatory wave.

Noncommercial broadcast entities, financed largely by viewer/listener fees or out of national general revenues, were previously afforded a degree of autonomy. They could escape, at least partly, advertising pressures. This was also the case with the national posts, telecommunications, and telegraph systems. They could, and did, impose conditions on the transnational companies that were compelled to use their services. This autonomy has vanished with the appearance of the new information technologies. In the changed global scene, the view of the International Advertising Association (IAA), representative of the interests of international advertising agencies and their transnational corporate sponsors, is a valuable guide to current developments.

Until recently, the international advertisers and their transnational corporate clients were chafing at the limited access granted them over national broadcast systems in France, Italy, England, Germany, and Western Europe in general. (Eastern Europe and the Soviet Union, until the arrival of *perestroika* and *glasnost,* were relatively virgin areas to the advertising folk. Now Pepsi commercials float across Soviet TV screens.) In the mid-1980s, the IAA assessed the situation and found it well on the way to improvement:

> Broadcasters have long had the technical resources to reach the whole world with commercial signals but many political, economic and social barriers made such services impractical. Now those barriers are being splintered and scattered by irresistible technological innovations and the social, political and economic repositioning that follow.[16]

Elaborating the new conditions, the IAA report adds:

> The magical *marketing tool of television* has been bound with the chains
> of laws and regulations, in much of the world, and it has not been free to
> exercise more than a tiny fraction of its potential as a conduit of the
> consumer information [sic] and economic stimulation provided by adver-
> tising. Those chains are at last being chiseled off. Irreversible forces are
> at work to vastly increase commercial television in Europe and around
> the world. There will be new commercial channels and far fewer restric-
> tions on existing advertising media.[17]

What are these "irreversible forces" that are "liberating" European
and world television and, at the same time, enabling them to become
conduits of commercialism and consumerism? One primary force is the
steadily expanding role and influence of the transnational corporation
and its supporters in the business and government sectors of each
individual nation. Another is the development of the new information
technologies. These enable the corporate sector to threaten to bypass
national broadcast and telecommunications entities entirely. The new
information capabilities allow the establishment of free-standing facilities accessible to anyone who can afford to pay for them—who other
than the resource-rich transnational companies? This capability was
the preferred means of exerting pressure on the once-monopolistic
market position of AT&T in the United States. The threat is forceful
and difficult to ignore: yield or be abandoned! This tactic is being
applied in Europe and elsewhere. It is facilitated immeasurably by
playing off one nation against another. For example, once the English
privatized and deregulated, large corporations operating in other European states threatened to transfer their activities to Britain unless
they could obtain similar conditions wherever they were.

These threats are made credible by the flexibility of the new information technologies which permit the relocation of enterprise and the
shifting of capital and labor without too much cost and little fuss.
Actually, it is not altogether a new practice. Throughout capitalist
development, domestically and internationally, production shifted to
where the advantage to capital was maximal. Today, it is simply more
a matter of degree.

In the broadcast field, there is a new wrinkle introduced by the use of
satellite communications and cable systems. If a national broadcasting
system, for example, should resist privatization and commercialization
and the widespread sale of advertising time, the national authority may
be circumvented. Advertisers may resort to communication-satellite

transmission, enabling their sales messages and programming to be picked up on local sets or by national cable systems. In either case, the national audience is exposed to the message but the advertising revenues will be pocketed by those outside the national jurisdiction.

Short of shooting the satellites out of the sky or refusing to introduce cable systems, national authorities are in a bind. Their only alternative, which seemingly has little appeal, is to allocate significantly increased shares of national tax revenues to the noncommercial system. Though there is increasing recognition of the importance of the national cultural sphere, it is not yet seen as the equivalent of the more narrowly defined economic sector. This, of course is a serious strategic mistake and plays directly into the hands of the transnational corporate order. Consequently, the chances of avoiding penetration and ultimate takeover by transnational corporate culture grow progressively slimmer.

Transnational Corporate Culture's New Frontiers

The experience of recent years bears out this analysis. The penetration and expansion of transnational corporate products and practices in Europe and the rest of the world have been deep and multilayered. Already, in many places the new culture is regarded as "natural," no longer an intrusion that provokes dismay or opposition.

There are many elements in this new culture. The source and style of television programming is the most visible and identifiable feature, but it is by no means its exclusive characteristic. Also affected by transnational corporate influence are national politics, sports, tourism, language, and many kinds of information flows.

The signs of corporate culture, not surprisingly, are most observable in the older, industrially developed societies of Western Europe. These are nations in which powerful domestic enterprises, as well as transnational companies, are based. They fully support and utilize the techniques and practices of their transatlantic (and transpacific) competitors—and ofttimes, collaborators.

The once-independent national broadcasting systems of France, Italy, and England have been privatized and commercialized in varying degree. Most other European systems also are succumbing to transnational corporate pressure, though a few fight delaying actions. *Business Week* reports on this deregulation:

> As deregulation sweeps Western Europe . . . makers of consumer goods are rethinking their marketing plans to reach mass audiences as never before. This could mean a heyday for international advertising.[18]

Similarly, the senior vice president of CBS Broadcast International notes that "Europe is clearly the fastest growing market in the world [for commercial television]."[19] The implication of this was matter-of-factly assessed in *Variety's 1986 International Television Annual:* " . . . the historical concept that a nation can control the shape and content of broadcast media is out the window."[20]

This poses an interesting question. If a nation's responsible authorities are unable to administer the most powerful educational force in society—TV—who has this mandate? As things are turning out, this role, with its hard-to-exaggerate importance, increasingly is being fulfilled by transnational companies. Already, the international advertising industry is salivating as European television goes commercial. It is expected by Saatchi & Saatchi, the advertising superagency, that "European broadcast advertising will jump 56 percent to $12.5 billion by 1990,"[21] from $5.8 billion in 1987. And the best is yet to come.

By mid-1987, *Business Week* could report that "The Media Barons Battle to Dominate Europe as deregulation sweeps the television industry."[22] This communiqué, in effect, announced that the transnational corporate offensive against national control of media and culture had been successful. The current period is concerned with media combines fighting and dealing among themselves for shares in the world market and the global-TV-profit pie.

Rupert Murdoch, the Australian-American media tycoon, has been especially busy. He plans to beam four TV channels to British homes in 1989 from a satellite and is exulting, "We are seeing the dawn of an age of freedom in viewing and advertising."[23] Murdoch's astonishing 1988 buyout of Annenberg media interests, including *TV Guide,* is part of his vision for promoting global advertising, managed by a global communications company.[24]

The situations in Italy and France further exemplify the present state of affairs and how the battle has gone. The Italian commercial-TV impressario, Silvio Berlusconi—to whom *Variety's 17th International Television Annual* devoted dozens of laudatory pages, "alone raked in about $1 billion for advertising in 1986."[25] This accomplishment was facilitated by a huge importation of American programming, "an extraordinary 70 percent of Italian TV is imported."[26] Berlusconi's profits also were affected greatly by saturating the Italian home screens with 16–18 minutes of commercials per hour. To give an idea of what a deluge of commercialism this represents, American television, whose producers have enshrined the commercial, carries "only" half that amount in prime time.

Italy's full-scale participation in transnational corporate culture goes beyond importing U.S. TV programs. Another indicator is the announcement that "a fantasy-theme park similar to Disneyland is to be built on Italy's northeast Adriatic coast."[27] So much for the birthplace of the Renaissance and the home of opera! Yet apparently to some Eastern European states, developments in Italy are promising. Perhaps a sign of things to come in that region of the world is the news that Poland has contracted to receive in late 1988 transmission from Italy's principal state TV network—a structure itself deeply penetrated by U.S. programming.[28]

Given the historical national concern with the defense and promotion of French culture, capitulation in that country to transnational media and cultural products is still more astonishing than in Italy. Not so long ago, a French minister of culture, Jack Lang, to the cheers of an international audience at a UNESCO-sponsored conference in Mexico City, castigated American cultural and financial imperialism. Lang did not put quotation marks around these terms. He also carefully distinguished between artistic creativity and the outputs of the cultural industries.[29]

In 1987, a few years later, a different French minister of culture, François Léotard, found much to admire in the U.S. cultural scene— so much so, that he intended to introduce into France the highly developed corporate-cultural interlocks that are so prominent in the American social landscape. In fact, these are the connections that have allowed the widespread inroads of corporate influence over American creative energies. "I want to bring in additional partners," Léotard explained, "to get the private sector involved—corporations, localities, private citizens . . . "[30]

Taking one step in that direction, the Louvre has recently announced that it is "seek[ing] American corporate and private financing to help complete a decade-long project to renovate the museum and upgrade its conservation and exhibition facilities."[31] Should the Louvre's solicitation be successful, can one expect to see over the portals of that venerable institution, as over the doors of several American museums, "open Tuesday nights by courtesy of Mobil, Exxon, Philip Morris," or some other corporate donor?

Léotard also wanted in his brief tenure, which lasted to the 1988 Mitterand presidential victory, to "disengage the Government from television bit by bit." He recognized that this could not be achieved overnight. "The mind-set of the French public is something that has to be changed over a period of time."[32] As this is precisely what corporate culture seeks to do—change the public's mind-set—it is evident that the minister was following the appropriate course in his choice of partners and instruments.

Meanwhile, with three of its television channels privatized, France is beginning to experience the "pleasures" of fully commercialized entertainment. This extends to the type of programs produced and screened, the creation of the star personality, the rating wars, and the rest of the frenetic money-making atmosphere that permeates American TV culture.

The takeover by corporate culture in France is described by one French TV executive as "a great period of modernization."[33] This calls to mind the exhortations of American policy-makers to Third World leaders to "modernize" and become "entrepreneurial." "Indeed," as a *Wall Street Journal* reporter saw it, "capitalism has come to French television with a vengeance."[34] This assessment was endorsed enthusiastically by the chairman of the National Commission for Communication and Freedom, a creation of the late conservative Chirac government. Gabriel de Broglie exclaimed: "We have given birth to a free enterprise audiovisual world."[35]

What are the characteristics of this free-enterprise, audiovisual world? First, the *New York Times* reports, " . . . the time authorized by the supposedly independent public communications authority for commercials has gone from 18 minutes *a day* in 1985 to 12 minutes *an hour* in 1987."[36] Additionally, the onetime European disbelief of and contempt for American TV shows that are incessantly interrupted by commercials has been replaced by "realism." "Starting now," an official of the recently privatized network TF 1 has been quoted as saying, "the producers who want to work for us know that their productions will be cut up. So do the viewers."[37]

Bidding wars between the private channels for stars and programs are raging. One channel offers more than another for *Dallas*—the loser gets the rights to screen *Knots Landing*. French creativity loses, and the audience views another nighttime soap opera churned out either by American cultural factories or their French imitators.

And there is more from where *Dallas* and *Knots Landing* came. Hollywood's vaults are filled with old films. For example, 2,500 "oldies" came under the control of Rupert Murdoch when he purchased 20th Century-Fox. They are expected to become one of the main sources of programming for the cable systems operating in Europe and being constructed in many other countries. According to *Business Week:*

With increasing deregulation of television in Europe, and with cable systems expanding, broadcasting and cable operators are hungry for programming. At the same time, U.S. and foreign advertisers are eager to reach European consumers.[38]

Not only are U.S. films and TV series flickering across French, Italian, and other European screens; corporate network news programs from the United States are also transmitted (in their original format) to transatlantic audiences. *CBS Evening News* with Dan Rather comes on the air in France the morning after its evening presentation in the United States. Japan's NHK airs ABC's *World News Tonight.* Cable News Network (CNN) at the end of 1987 claimed to serve 61 countries in Europe and elsewhere, including 113 hotels in Western Europe.[39] Most of these news programs are aimed at the "English-speaking population in the business and professional world outside the United States." They are transmitted to reach the transnational corporate executive and salaried personnel outside the United States. This is a growing and "demographically desirable" audience. It is an affluent group, ready to acquire what the accompanying commercials (to the programs) promote.

U.S. cultural industries are gearing up to exploit the world-market demand for equipment, expertise, and programming. U.S. data, films, television shows, news, and recorded music flood the international market. Patrick J. Leahy, chairman of the Senate Judiciary Committee's Subcommittee on Technology and the Law, observed that "While other economic sectors show steady deficits, the makers of American books, computer software, recordings, movies and other copyrighted materials . . . generated a $1.5 billion trade surplus" in 1987.[40]

Yet there is more to this than a busy traffic in cultural products. As TV and film production costs escalate in the United States, the world market becomes increasingly vital to American producers. Without it, most productions would not be profitable. Domestic deficits—the difference between what it costs to produce a TV show, for example, and what the producer receives from the networks to whom it is sold—are made up increasingly by sales in the international market. Already, U.S. producers account for 79 percent of global film and television exports.[41]

Given this production dilemma, markets beyond the familiar Western European outlets are being cultivated. The Chinese market, fabulous in potential, is being given much attention. "The studios are dealing with China primarily to see if it will develop into the huge and profitable market that peddlers . . . have dreamed of since . . . the early 1970s."[42] It is realized that the payoff is distant. The long-term potential is motivating the studios' present discount and unprofitable movie sales to China. Current wheeling and dealing in American media properties reflect these anticipations.

The Total Corporate Information-Cultural Environment

What is happening in Europe and elsewhere represents far more than a continuation of heavy importation of Anglo-American media materials and the exposure of local audiences to this inflow. It constitutes a totally new dimension of transnational corporate influence. In the 1960s and 1970s media flows were already a troubling issue, especially in the newly decolonized parts of the world. Asian, African, and Latin American countries raised objections to the one-way flow of media products—films, TV programs, news, books, recordings—from a few Western centers into their national space.

Today the situation has been transformed. *All* geographical areas are affected. The cultural-informational sector no longer is a matter of concern only to the poorer societies. What is now happening is the creation and global extension of a near-total corporate informational-cultural environment.

Familiar media products continue to be an important component of this environment. But these comprise only a part of a larger and far more comprehensive package. Now, a huge volume of electronic data hurtles through space—almost completely outside of national oversight—the so-called transborder data flows. They may include such a benign item as travel reservations. Yet they also carry the data essential to the national economy: banking and insurance transactions, engineering and architectural design, business operational information. For example, 3,700 on-line data bases in the United States offer—at a price—an all-inclusive package of a corporate economy's basic data, perspectives, and paradigms. Similarly, computer software programs, now a considerable export item, embody deep-structured corporate approaches to the organization of knowledge and problem-solving in general. In 1987, IBM sold $6.8 billion in copyrighted computer programs.[43]

The essential point is that an entire broadcast, informational, and cultural system, privately owned and managed, often helped by government policy but mainly dependent on transnational advertising on behalf of corporate sponsors (or corporate users in the case of electronic data flows), is being set in place. When such a system is consolidated, the utility of analyzing the effects of *one* program or medium is futile. The entire social mechanism has been transformed into a corporate exhibit or channel.

The process is no longer an exclusively American transnational corporate phenomenon either. The same mechanisms are available to whichever corporate system has the financial strength to introduce and utilize them. *Business Week* calls attention to the tactics employed by Japanese big business to win support in the United States. "Japanese companies are spending heavily," the magazine reports, "to shape the way Americans view them." *Business Week* estimates that in 1988 "Japan's government, foundations and companies will spend [excluding advertising outlays] at least $310 million . . . on soft-side activities." These activities include: contributions to the Children's Television Workshop, to influential American think tanks (The Brookings Institution, The American Enterprise Institute), to universities, and for exchange programs, education, and libraries. In addition, there is an estimated $45-million-a-year outlay on public relations. What do the Japanese hope to secure from this expensive and wide-reaching effort? "Most of all," *Business Week* explains, "Japan wants to maintain a political and economic status quo to prevent surprises from threatening its economic stake."[44]

Other Displays in the Corporate Exhibition Hall: Sports

The transnational corporate order's use of commercialized and privatized media to increase sales, create consumers, and transmit a mind-set supportive of the system is especially evident in the sphere of organized sports. As with many marketing practices, the commercialization of sport is an American speciality, rapidly being extended to the rest of the world. The Superbowl serves as the model. In this professional football extravaganza, promoted beforehand for months in all the media, the marketing message reaches half the American population, an estimated 125,000,000 viewers. The payoff of the carefully constructed frenzy preceding the game is the cost of a 30-second commercial during the game—$625,000 to $675,000 in 1987. For this amount, beer, automobile, insurance, and cosmetic companies get their product seen by half the country's population. It is, in the words of one sports writer, "the great corporate event."[45]

It is reported that "more than 3,400 U.S. companies (in 1987) will spend $1.35 billion to sponsor sporting events. . . . They'll spend another $500 million hiring athletes as (product) endorsers. . . . Along with ads and promotions directly tied to sponsorship, the amount may top $3.5 billion, or more than double the $1.4 billion in revenues the networks receive from selling ads during sports shows."[46]

Meanwhile, a new twist has been added in the current era of "total" marketing. Advertisers now may sponsor the sporting event itself rather than just buying a chunk of airtime during the show. The internationalization of this practice is already substantial. Transnational corporations committed at least $300 million to support the 1988 Olympic Games in Calgary and Seoul. Though the Olympics are still short of full corporate appropriation, the giant sums already involved suggest total envelopment may not be far off. Even now, the Olympics are regarded by corporate sponsors, "as a marketing tool throughout the world."[47] In 1994, the World Cup soccer tournament, one of world's premier sporting events, will be held in the United States, though soccer is not a major sport in America. To secure the tournament, the U.S. bid "enlisted help from eight American-based corporations, most of them multinational companies and three of them—Anheuser Busch, Gillette and Coca-Cola, sponsors of the 1990 tournament [in Italy]."[48]

In privatized broadcasting systems, corporate-sponsored sports are a large and growing source of revenue, bearing many similarities to the corporate-sponsored art exhibit or, more grandiose still, the corporate-sponsored museum. An American sports promotion company, for example, has created among its many commercialized sports packages for sale to corporate clients twenty European gold tournaments.[49]

Grand Prix automobile racing also is getting corporate attention. "Executives of the (Data General Corporation) say (its) involvement in racing helps to open the doors for salesmen overseas and enhances its reputation as a high-tech problem solver."[50] Philip Morris has used the Grand Prix since 1972, and R. J. Reynolds, another major cigarette company, joined the crowd of sponsors in 1987.

With the capture of sports for corporate promotions, the audience is targeted in its most vulnerable condition, relaxed yet fully receptive to the physical action and the inserted sales pitch. It is the ideal ambiance for the penetration of consciousness by a wide variety of ideological messages.

Media Politics—Another Room in the Corporate Exhibition Hall

Once the informational structure has been privatized and commercial-ized, it becomes an integral part of the political system as well, profit-ing from the new techniques it makes available to the electoral pro-cess and transforming the process at the same time. Commercial broadcasting encourages political parties to package and sell their candidates, just as automobiles and beer are marketed. It is not the cause of this phenomenon, but it is a remarkable facilitator.

In addition to providing substantial revenues to the media owners from the sale of time (or space), commercial broadcasting insures also that only candidates with ample resources can obtain adequate access to the media. The staggering sums that are required to pay for TV time can come either from the candidate's personal fortune or (mostly) from corporate treasuries. Individual contributions are, for the most part, secondary, except for the big donations. (These are actually corporate-related and are hardly to be considered "grass-roots" contributions.)

Corporate funding is the basic legitimizer in the contemporary elec-toral process. Accordingly, it compels the candidate to pass a corpo-rate litmus test of political and economic reliability. The primaries provide the popularity screening. The corporate sector, to the extent possible, favors candidates with personalities acceptable to the voters.

In any case, the main point is that large sums of money are the prerequisite for running and being elected to office in modern market economies. The pattern that was initiated and developed in the United States is now being replicated in many parts of the world. With the deregulation and privatizing of broadcasting, the American style of media electioneering has become the standard in Western Europe (also in Latin America and elsewhere) as some recent electoral cam-paigns reveal. A report on Italy, for example, noted: " . . . television overtook instinctive politics in the last general election in 1983. That was the first nationwide campaign held after new laws that allowed for a proliferation of private television stations around the country, ripe for use by politicians."[51] *cf. the recent decline of the very popular I.t communist party.*

This, in turn, has paved the way for the appearance of a retinue of image-making specialists who now oversee a candidate's campaign presentation, along with media consultants, pollsters, fund-raisers, public-relations and marketing types. In Spain, *Business Week* reported, "The victory of Socialist Prime Minister Felipe Gonzalez (in June 1987) was as much a media coup as a political event."

What explains this European-wide political transformation? *Business Week* attributes it to deregulation of communications:

> One of the most important reasons for the shift in campaign tactics is the growing deregulation of Europe's airwaves. As state monopolies [sic] of television and radio are dismantled, access to the media is putting powerful—indeed essential new tools into the hands of politicians.[52]

This is almost, but not quite right. Access to the deregulated media is not only "putting powerful new tools into the hands of politicians," but it is also putting politicians and political parties—to a greater extent than before—into the hands of corporate power. It is only the corporate sector that can finance the candidates' indispensable access to the media.

In the meantime, "a growing crop of U.S. political consultants . . . are emerging in Europe." This is probably a passing phenomenon. In fact, the same report notes that "A doctoral program in communications at the Sorbonne in Paris attracted 10 applicants for every place this year.(1986)"[53] No doubt about it! The Europeans, as well as the Latin Americans and the Asians, eventually will train and produce their own media specialists. Media politics is not a nationality issue. It is an outcome of the transformation of basic national infrastructures into more serviceable institutions for transnational corporate capital.

Lamenting, therefore, the vulgarity, manipulation, simple-mindedness, and reductionist thinking and programming that characterize media campaigning is really beside the point. These are precisely the techniques that make for effective TV marketing. This is what is intended. It is the advice supplied by the swelling number of media consultants, whatever their national origin. In a corporate-underwritten culture, why should politics and candidates be treated differently than other commodities for sale? Call it cultural imperialism or what you will. What is apparent is that "modern" media politics are the inseparable accompaniments of transnational corporate economy and culture.

A World Secure for Global Advertising?

The Global Media Commission of the International Advertising Association anticipates the future with enthusiasm and optimism. This may be customary with marketing folk. Is there a basis for this confidence? As the ad people see it, " . . . television, that most efficient and spectacularly effective of all mass media, will soon be available to serve as global marketing's instrument of consumer access."[54] It will be transmitted by satellite and delivered to cable systems, bringing advertising and programming to audiences whether their governments like it or not, compelling national systems to accept commercialization to survive. And so, " . . . the state monopolies [the favorite negative language employed by the experts of the transnationals] will be able to survive only by competing. The number of channels will multiply. Private television will grow. Advertising time will expand and flourish in both private and public broadcasting systems."[55] Transnational corporate culture will be triumphant. There is, the admen believe, "an inexorable momentum."[56]

It is difficult to disagree. The global push of transnational capital in the information-cultural sphere has been remarkably successful to date. No activity, national or international, is exempt from the corporate sponsor—not even, apparently, the worldwide programs of the United Nations. This is the message delivered by a highly placed UN official to the World Congress on Public Relations in Melbourne, Australia, in April 1988. The UN's under-secretary for public information told the congress:

> A critical component in my new approach is to explore corporate and institutional sponsorship. Recently we have started to work with corporations in putting the UN message across to the people of the world . . . We have realized that both [PR] agencies and their clients would benefit substantially in corporate image terms in their association with us and the work that we do. . . . a particularly attractive opportunity for sponsorship is the 40th anniversary of the *United Nations Declaration of Human Rights in 1988* . . . the opportunities for joint promotion are as wide as the United Nations global network around the world.[57]

With this invitation, corporate sponsorship could be magnificently expanded from Grand Prix and Olympics events to the United Nations itself. Imagine the commercials showing the U.S. fleet in the Persian Gulf as a UN event sponsored by Exxon. When asked why there should be subsidized national theater in England funded from the state treasury, Peter Hall, the British director, observed that a national theater had to be considered the last defense against U.S. commercial-television programming.[58]

But it is not only U.S. television programming that carries the virus of transnational corporate culture. Politics, sports, tourism, language, and business data flows transmit it and reinforce it as well. One event gives a sense of the process at work. It was a rock-band concert in Tijuana, just across the border from San Diego, California. The newspaper account of this concert attended by 27,000 people, a small turnout for such an event, noted: "While staged in Mexico, the concert scene could have been transplanted from the United States." Mexican national sovereignty was disregarded. "Some souvenir booths carried signs saying 'No Acceptamos Pesos'—we don't accept pesos." The reporter from Los Angeles reasonably concluded: "The theme of cross-cultural cooperation apparently did not extend to accepting the Mexican national currency on Mexican soil."[59]

The African novelist and essayist, Ngugi wa Thiong'o, in exile because his native Kenya is a domain of transnational capital, summed up the consequences of cultural subjugation:

> But the biggest weapon wielded and actually daily unleashed by imperialism against collective defiance [of the oppressed and exploited] is the cultural bomb. The effect of the cultural bomb is to annihilate a people's belief in their names, in their languages, in their environment, in their heritage of struggle, in their unity, in their capacities and ultimately in themselves.[60]

Ngugi wa Thiong'o was writing with his African brothers and sisters in mind. The conditions of the Asian, African, and Latin American peoples cannot be equated with those of the Europeans. Still, making allowance for national specificities and differing levels of material development, the "cultural bomb" has much the same effect wherever it falls. Those things that prevent its use or can reduce its impact are discussed next.

|7|

Thinking About Media Power: Who Holds It? A Changing View

The industries that manufacture the messages and imagery that create the national and international cultural atmosphere have grown greatly in size, breadth, and productive capability in the years since World War II. Expanding, merging, and transnationalizing, these industries now represent an awesome concentration of cultural power and influence, at home and in the world at large. Additionally, they increasingly constitute a significant component of the general economy. Number of workers employed, value of output, connection to industrial processes and management, and exports as a growing share of the balance of trade attest to the cultural industries' greater importance in national life.

Actually, reliance on information and data may be the most salient characteristic of capitalist enterprise and governance in the current period. This largely accounts also for the evolution of the legal status of commercial and corporate speech. This status has changed in half a century from near-prohibition to almost full constitutional protection.

Given these far-reaching and structural changes in the economy and the transformations of legal doctrine that facilitate the full utilization of communication power by the corporate order, it is puzzling, if not astonishing, to note the prevailing assessment of media's capability to influence people and events. While the actual holders of economic and political authority resort increasingly to one or another form of communication to further extend or at least reinforce their influence, current theorists writing about communication find media influence highly overrated. For the most part, they view the media as more subject to audience preferences than to its own material interests and imperatives.

Yet those who theorize about the media and the communication process did not always have this view, or, at least, it was not the only view in town. In fact, critical as well as mainstream scholars and writers agree that three fairly distinct periods over the last half-century can be identified in the changing view of media power: the twenty years or so after World War II; the upheaval decade of the mid-'60s to the mid-'70s; and the "restoration" era from the end of the '70s to the present—where market rules dominate and capital-holders have enjoyed almost unrestricted privileges. The agreement ends with the identification of the three periods.

Period 1: The First Two Decades (1945–65)

Two markedly different readings of media power come into play in the first period, the two decades after the war. One view is given a clear presentation by Elihu Katz, a major figure in communication research for forty years. Katz traces the current appreciation of the "limited effects" of media back to the pioneer communication research of Paul Lazarsfeld and his group (including Katz) at Columbia University, undertaken in the early 1940s.

From that work came the so-called "dominant paradigm" of communication research. It emphasized the limited effects of the media, stressing instead processes of individual selectivity, perception, and recall. Katz (rightly, in my view) sees this work as the predecessor of subsequent studies that concentrated on what the receiver (the audience) either brought to or how it utilized the message. These included studies on "uses and gratifications," diffusion of innovations, and, most recently, network and decoding analysis. Katz sees these efforts as direct descendants of the original "limited-effects" paradigm, initially formulated by Lazarsfeld et al.[1]

Katz and his colleagues, however, pay little or no attention to the work and perspectives of those who were concerned with the global arena and to the role of mass communication in securing the political attachment of people outside the United States, especially those in the newly decolonized regions. These were well aware of—and strongly supported—the world expansionist role of the United States, the efforts of the American media in particular, in the postwar period.

In this circle, largely centered at the Massachusetts Institute of Technology (MIT), the evaluation of media power differed sharply from that of the Lazarsfeld contingent. At MIT, the basic assumption was that the media, and communication in general, were powerful agents of social change. As such they could be utilized in promoting the development of the newly independent nations of Asia and Africa along lines acceptable to and of benefit to Western private enterprise. Though not the subject of their attention, the domestic use of the media as the superlative instrument of marketing constituted the basis for their optimism for its international use and application.

Thus, while the "limited-effects" model of the media prevailed at home—though not without some troublesome aspects*—the appearance of new fields, international communication and its twin, development communication, seemed validation enough of the assumption of actual media power. At the same time, the creation of these new areas of research and policy-making highlighted the close cooperation between the theorists and political organizers of the postwar international economy—then in its formative stage.

Bulking large in U.S. policy-making in the early postwar era were two vital and inseparable objectives: to halt and push back, if possible, the growth of nonmarket (socialist) states; and to integrate as quickly as possible the rest of the world into an international market economy dominated by the United States.

In striving for these ends, the use of communication, especially international communication, was seen as indispensable. The contribution of communication scholarship to the theoretical models that supported and gave thrust to American policy was considerable. In this work, the importance of communication and the mass media were viewed as central.

The work of Daniel Lerner is exemplary. Lerner, along with Wilbur Schramm, Ithiel de Sola Pool, Lucien Pye, et al., constituted the group of American communication academics who at the time were providing the analytical spine and the texts of U.S. policy—and offering an alternative to the Lazarsfeld finding that media did not possess undue power to influence. Lerner was among the first to grasp and articulate the geopolitical strategy of securing the excolonial world

---

*Katz is not unaware of the ideological usefulness of the "limited-effects" finding of the media studies. "For years," he writes, "researchers in these traditions [campaign diffusion, gratifications research] played a debunking role: the power of the media is overrated, they said, and they returned some part of the power to the audience." Katz acknowledged that these findings were pleasing to media controllers and exonerated them from accountability and blame.[2] This conclusion is as true in 1989 as it was in 1950.

for Western-structured "development." In doing so, he helped found
the new field of development communication that incorporated this
strategy into its underlying assumptions and practices. In a 1977 volume which undertook a half-century appraisal of communication research, Lerner looked back on the origins of the association of communication with development. He wrote:

> "Development" as an international ideology began with a
> communication—the State of the Union message delivered to Congress
> by President Harry S Truman in January 1949

Lerner singled out the key portion, in his estimation, of the address:

> The fourth point of President Truman's message announced a "bold new
> program" of United States technical assistance and financial aid to poor
> countries around the world. This policy, which became known as "Point
> IV", was soon adopted by other rich countries, as well as by regional and
> international organizations. Thus came into operation the development
> paradigm—aid from richer to poorer countries—that has been a major
> factor in the world political process over the past quarter-century.[3]

Fortune magazine, at the time of the program's announcement, not
quite as sanguine as Lerner about the proposal's humanism, labeled it
a "great international propaganda victory."[4] Yet Lerner was correct
in emphasizing the proposal's importance. He recognized that the
inspiration for the program and the objective it was intended to serve
were bound up with "(1) decline of Europe as the world power center; (2) bipolarization and domination of the world by the two nuclear
super powers; and, (3) emergence of the Third World."[5]

Lerner also understood that it was the "emergence of the Third
World" that constituted the grand prize at stake, holding the key to the
long-term viability of the world-market system. "The passing of European imperialism," he wrote, "entailed the emergence of new nations
as former colonies became independent political entities. The end of tu-
telage required the start of training for self-management. In this sense,
postwar decolonization was the source of development ideology and
procedure."[6] Accordingly, Lerner and his colleagues joined whole-
heartedly in supporting the U.S. Point IV program for the "development" of the new nations. In doing so, they formulated a number of
communication/development theorems that were intended to smooth
the process.

The Point IV program, however, was not the unalloyed, generous enterprise it was publicized to be. Coming immediately in the wake of the Marshall Plan first announced in 1947, which successfully preserved Western Europe's institutional structure at the end of the war, Point IV was the mechanism created either to introduce market forces into the excolonial world or strengthen them if they already were present.

In truth, Truman's 1949 inaugural address, which contains the Point IV proposal in its concluding recommendation, was essentially an anticommunist diatribe that purported to demonstrate the disaster that would accompany a nation's decision to deviate from a market-directed economy. Truman also assured the new nations that the proposed program had nothing in common with practices with which they were all too familiar:

> The old imperialism—exploitation for foreign profit—has no place in our plans. What we envisage is a program of development based on the concepts of democratic fair-dealing.[7]

Years later, Lerner repeated Truman's assertion about the demise of imperialism. He supplemented it with a communication dimension that became the model for the field of development communication. According to Lerner:

> The long era of imperialism (subordination) is recently ended: the campaign for international development (equalization) has just begun. In the new process, international communication operates in behalf of different policy purposes under different socio-economic conditions by different psychopolitical means. Indeed, in the transition from imperialism to international development, there has been a fundamental change in the role of communication. Under the new conditions of globalism, it has largely replaced the coercive means by which colonial territories were seized and held. . . . . *The persuasive transmission of enlightenment is the modern paradigm of international communication.*[8]

Lerner disregarded a mountain of evidence that contradicted his and Truman's comforting assurances that imperialism was dead and that "equalization" was the new goal of Western policy.

The interest here is the emphasis that was placed on communication. Despite the Lazarsfeld-Katz paradigm of "limited-effects," the thesis Lerner propagated dominated the thinking of government policy—to say nothing of domestic media usage—for at least two decades after the war's end.

Lerner's special talent rested in his recognition of the key role communication might (and did) play in the creation of an international market economy in which the United States occupied the center of the system. In Lerner's prescription, there is a "transition from coercion to communication."[9] Actually, even this much-to-be-desired development has been applicable or evident only if the excolonial entity settled for a market economy and allowed itself to be incorporated into the dominant world business order. In those instances where new states have insisted on some measure of autonomy in the selection and operation of their socioeconomic systems, they have encountered unrelenting coercion—economic, military, and cultural. Maps locating the dozens of direct interventions, coups, and economic blockades instituted and enforced by U.S. power over the last forty years could almost fill an Atlas. However, once a region has been "stabilized," the utilization of international communication has provided an essential means for "harmonizing" the operations and routines of the world commercial economy with the area.

The media ratios that American communication specialists used to delight in calculating to express levels of a society's development, e.g., cinema seats per hundred (of the population), newspaper readership, radio sets per capita, etc., however overblown in importance, did, in fact, though not intentionally, measure one important condition—the extent to which a country had been propelled into the global market system and, relatedly, how deeply it had been penetrated by mostly American media products and services. The ratios were an excellent measure of the extent to which the "persuasive transmission of enlightenment" was occurring.

Lerner, displaying a humorous side, appropriated Karl Marx as an early proponent of development-communication theory. Culling one sentence from *Das Kapital,* "The more developed society presents to the less developed society *a picture of its own future.*" Lerner used this fragment to produce an endorsement of his own paradigm. Lerner felt Marx took the wrong road when he did not work out more thoroughly this one aperçu:

Unfortunately, for Marx and for the poorer areas of the world, he never persisted in the exploration of his own insight. Had he done so, he might be known today as the "father of international communication," surely a more constructive role than "father of international communism" with its predictions of international war and prescriptions of global class conflict.[10]

Period 2: International and Domestic Challenges to the U.S. Cultural Industries—The Demand for a New International Information Order and Social Turbulence at Home.

Lerner, Schramm, Pool, and other American communication scholars—leaving aside the "limited-effects" contingent, which was probably a majority of the field—had no doubt that the modern media and the new information technologies were means of great potential influence. The world provided a laboratory in which their views were tested. For twenty years, U.S. and English media products and services flowed across national boundaries and into places at one time sealed off by various protective practices. The effect of this torrential cultural flow was the creation in the postwar years of a world information order structured largely by American cultural industries. More than media activities were involved. U.S. business, taking advantage of the war-ravaged Western economies, established itself as the dominant force on the European continent and elsewhere.

The U.S. media participated vigorously in this expansionist wave. The Associated Press and United Press International, for example, dislodged Reuters and the other European news agencies as the primary suppliers of international news. Since then, the world has been reported largely through the eyes of American-owned news organizations. Hollywood films, with considerable assistance from the Motion Picture Export Association, saturated the world's movie screens. In the 1950s and early 1960s, American television programs, replete with images of U.S. products and services, became fare of viewers all over the world. U.S. tourists, advertising, popular music, books (especially school texts), magazines, and the extent of the English language itself, contributed to the making of a transnational commercial culture.

Many in the United Nations, and in UNESCO especially, saw those developments as encouraging signs of progress in the poorer countries. UNESCO reports, written by U.S. communication experts in those days, generally claimed that the mass media and the products they advertised provided the motivation for what was approvingly called "modernization." This meant adopting, as rapidly as possible, the basic features of private enterprise. American communication experts were correct in pointing out that the mass media played an important role in that process. If the goal of modernization was the consumer society, the United States provided the model, and the American mass media celebrated and promoted it.

During this period, UNESCO, at the urging of the United States, also endorsed a principle that underlay and ennobled the expansion of the American cultural industries. This was the doctrine of the "free flow of information." Unexceptional and even highly desirable as an abstract standard, in practice the free-flow idea gave a green light for the global penetration of the products of U.S. media-cultural conglomerates like CBS, Time, Inc., J. Walter Thompson, 20th Century-Fox and others. Any nation's effort to regulate that flow was sternly rejected as tantamount to totalitarianism.

No less convinced than the American communications scholars of the influence of media on their social existence, the newly independent nations, now a majority in international organizations, began to make public their criticisms of the cultural domination they believed they were experiencing. As early as an Algiers conference in 1973, the leaders of the nonaligned movement—mostly countries from Asia, Africa, and Latin America—issued a strong statement to that effect:

> It is an established fact that the activities of imperialism are not confined solely to the political and economic fields but also cover the cultural and social fields, thus imposing an alien ideological domination over the peoples of the developing world.[11]

At a number of international meetings of UN bodies and Third World nations in the mid-1970s, the characteristics and extent of the Western information monopoly were discussed. The one-way flows of news from a few Western centers drew special criticism. Gatherings were held in Quito, Lima, Bogota, Mexico City, San José, Tunis, Colombo, and New Delhi, among other cities. Although no specific new information order was promulgated at these meetings, three main demands emerged: greater variety in sources of information, less monopolization of the forms of cultural expression, and preservation of some national cultural space from the pervasive commercialization of Western cultural outpourings. From all these statements and meetings, there was left no doubt in the minds of Third World cultural figures that the products of the Western cultural industries had an effect on the peoples to whom they were targeted.

Recognition of the influence of and challenge to American and Western cultural industries did not come exclusively from the leaders of the new nations. At home, throughout most of the 1960s, domestic movements for civil rights, women's equality, protection of the environment, and the struggle against the war in Vietnam first objected to and then attempted to change the prevailing media representations—

on television, in film, over the radio, and in the press—of blacks, women, the war, and the meaning of nature.

Great efforts were exerted in the '60s to create new channels for popular expression that would admit of the possibility for social and institutional change. This was a time of alternative media, of the underground press (which was hardly underground and which at its peak numbered hundreds of papers). It was the era of guerrilla video and the portapak which enabled individuals to move with videocameras directly into the actual social scene. In these few years, the complicity of the U.S. cultural-media establishment with American reaction at home and abroad was repeatedly revealed and documented.

The power of the message and the power of those who controlled the message were illuminated and brought briefly to national attention. It was very difficult, if possible at all, to claim that the media had "limited effects" in this decade. Most of the social action was based on the assumption that media power existed—and had to be resisted. In his review of "media-effects" theorizing in the forty postwar years, Elihu Katz acknowledges that the 1960s forced a brief reversal in the acceptance of the dominant "limited-effects" paradigm. He writes: "The revival of conflict theory in social science, and of social criticism in the 1960s produced a major revival in criticism of the mass media and their alliance with power. The ideological effect was dusted off."[12] For a brief moment, questions were asked, for example, about who established the agenda of social discourse. This was the theory of agenda-setting. But the reversal was short-lived.

Period 3: The Re-Emergence of the Old Paradigm

The strength of the reformist social movements in the United States began to ebb as the 1960s decade came to a close. This coincided roughly with the shift of political power, signified in the Nixon presidency, and the return to fierce global competition in the international industrial arena. A resumption of no-nonsense toughness by big business in defense of markets and profits, in abeyance for twenty-five years, made itself felt quickly thereafter in the industrial and social spheres.

The international, mostly Third World, effort to change the global cultural pattern crested in the fall of 1976, at the 19th General Conference of UNESCO in Nairobi, Kenya.

At that meeting, the U.S. delegation was obliged to take note of the near unanimity of the opposition it faced and to acknowledge what up to that time Washington had denied routinely—that there were indeed international "information imbalances." It was also in Nairobi, however, that the United States, though seemingly defensive and faltering, laid out the course it would follow in deflecting and defusing the challenge to its worldwide information advantage. To placate advocates of change, the United States acceded to the appointment of an international commission to study communication problems. Known as the MacBride Commission—after its chair, Nobel and Lenin Prize winner Sean MacBride—it issued a useful report in 1980, *Many Voices, One World,* along with almost one hundred related monographs and studies. In addition, the United States volunteered to offer technological assistance to those nations that wanted to expand their communications capabilities. The technological gambit continues to be the preferred method of the United States for dealing with information issues at home and abroad. It works in two ways.

First, from the technological perspective, information inadequacy can be expressed in terms of physical volume—how many words, pictures, paragraphs, feet of tape, number of films, records, books are produced and distributed. Yet, far more significant is the quality and the substance of the imagery produced and provided. What counts are the institutional arrangements and standards that govern cultural production. In short, who decides? For what objective?

Second, the U.S. offer to provide technical assistance diverted the demand for a new information order to "technical solutions." More important, it laid the groundwork for another condition of information dependency, one based on technology. Global information and cultural domination and control in the late 1980s are grounded in the capability to manufacture the hardware of advanced technologies such as satellites and computers, the organization and administration of international communication networks, the construction and ownership of comprehensive electronic data banks, and the creation of the software that sets all the information activity in motion.

In the new international division of labor that is set up under the guidance and direction of the transnational business system, information generation, processing, transmission, and dissemination are vital. Information has become an essential component in the world business economy. The long-standing dominance of the Western media, therefore, has been augmented by the enormous power of the multinational corporate system. Additionally, the social forces that previously held that system to a minimal standard of accountability are less and less capable of doing so. The massive transmission of economic data across national borders by global corporations has greatly weakened local governments and businesses.

The nation-state finds its autonomy eroding before the enlarged capabilities of the big companies, which are deciding independently how vital resources will be allocated. Less-developed countries are practically helpless. Labor also suffers as big employers shift production, capital, and data around the world almost at will. Public broadcasting and national telecommunications systems in Western Europe and elsewhere are being privatized and deregulated as global capital brushes aside public need and social obligation. The United Nations and its affiliated bodies are circumvented, attacked, sometimes abandoned. The U.S. withdrawal from UNESCO in 1984 was one expression of current transnational corporate aggressiveness. The State Department's spokesman on the issue was not shy about saying so. He explained the action as a response to efforts "to develop normative standards that would impose restraints on Western media and restrict activities of transnational corporations."[13]

In sum, the call for a new information order to increase the number of voices in the global discourse has been set aside. Instead of the hoped-for openness, there is a corporate regimen. The International Advertising Association has provided the now commanding vision: "world-class products being sold by uniform advertising campaigns on commercial television around the world."[14]

The Return of the "Limited-Effects" Paradigm

Few in the late 1980s would dispute the central role of information in the ordering of the world economy and in the operations and processes of domestic political, economic, and cultural life. Media, data flow, and the new information technologies constitute the dynamic information sector of the American and the transnational economies. All the more remarkable, therefore, that at this same time there is a resurgence of thinking and theorizing about the media that subscribes to the old "limited-effects" view of its influence. More extraordinary still, the minimizing of media power now is extended to the international arena, a field that was barely considered in the analyses of the early "limited-effects" theorists.

In the late 1980s, the power of the Western cultural industries is more concentrated and formidable than ever; their outputs are more voluminous and widely circulated; and the transnational corporate system is totally dependent on information flows. Yet the prevailing interpretation sees media power as highly overrated and its international impact minimal. This revivified outlook enjoys strong support in and outside of the academy. It is well on the way to becoming the accepted wisdom across a wide range of disciplines. Its usefulness to existing power is obvious. It has other attractions as well.

Media power, in the updated version of the old "limited-effects" model, is more than balanced by *audience power*. To a large extent, the discussion centers on television, but the general analysis is applicable, with allowance for differing characteristics, to other media forms as well. Two main arguments currently support the proposition of an "active audience,"* one which is no longer (if it ever was) prisoner of a powerful cultural-message system. It is, in the eyes of its proponents, an audience capable of producing its own meanings and resisting those transmitted to it that it finds objectionable or irrelevant.

First, it is claimed, the new information technologies afford greater choice. The second support factor derives from an appraisal of the audience, which finds it heterogeneous, comprised of a large number of social subgroups, each with its own history, experience, and interests. Few will disagree that there are new communication technologies available and that the audience is hardly a monolithic mass. But what do we make of these observations?

Technology and the Active Audience

The case for a technologically facilitated audience freedom is simple and straightforward. In his book entitled *The Technologies of Freedom,*[16] the late scholar Ithiel de Sola Pool argues that the new technologies which are given so weighty a role are essentially multichannel cable systems and home video recorders. The former now are present in 50 percent of American homes. The latter are rapidly approaching a similar level of penetration. On the basis of these developments, some charge that "many popular and influential theories of the media's impact on society are insensitive to the implications of the new video technologies." These have, so the argument runs, "the net effect of opening the distribution system to potentially unlimited channel capacities."[17] For this reason, " . . . The televised

---

*We leave aside in this discussion the very telling point of one writer and artist, Martha Rosler, whose definition of "audience" as "consumers of spectacles" makes the very notion of an "active" audience an oxymoron.[15]

images consumed across our pluralistic [sic] society are becoming increasingly disparate . . . (and) theorists should recognize that viewers are, as never before, in a position to construct media environments that may be quite different from those of their neighbors."[18]

More enthusiastic still are recent press accounts. One states:

> Viewers, experts say are gaining control over the media. *No longer are they just passive recipients of what a few networks have to offer. They are active participants with a wide variety of choices* and the technology to jump easily from channel to channel, tape shows they would otherwise miss, watch movies not available on broadcast television and in general create their own, personalized programming schedules.[19]

The expanded number of channels and the use of home video recorders are producing, according to another study reported in the press,

> . . . a generation of more active viewers in the sense that they don't watch programs anymore: they watch pieces of programs . . . You can now put together your own program of fragments.

In the same account, another expert finds this trend promising:

> There may be advantages to what appears to be a lack of coherency. We are given pieces and asked to make out of them what we can.[20]

The "active audience," according to its technological boosters, is for the most part made up of button pushers and channel changers, a restless crowd, creating individualized viewing packages and becoming in the process an increasingly fragmented population. What derives from this collage of the current media scene is that fear of the influence of concentrated media power as a bogeyman is no longer (if it ever was) warranted. People may be distracted by or even surrounded with incoherent symbolic environments, but they are not being socially influenced. How can they be, since they are their own agents of selection?

Yet, what is the *actual* diversity that is available over multichannel systems? To what extent is it a conglomeration of old movies, syndicated reruns, news from the same two or three press agencies, and sports of every description? Has the sponsor disappeared from cable television? Is commercialism and consumerism absent? Where are the sharply drawn social dramas? Has not cable television, no less than the networks, been swallowed by the big information-cultural combines?

All the same, the technology-based view of an emancipated viewer, despite an enormous blindspot—the inability to locate where power actually is vested in the new technologies—holds open, at least, the possibility of effecting social change. But there is a very considerable "if"—if the instrumentation had different controllers. In fact, there have been some heartening instances of community participation through public-access channels. These, however, remain terribly limited, to say nothing of being constantly threatened with revocation by cable owners who find it outrageous to be compelled to yield the tiniest fraction of their revenue-producing facilities for community use.

The Audience as Producer of Meaning = WHY my senior thesis sucked.

Minimization of concentrated media power is much more subtly argued by those who, for the most part, ignore the impact of the new technologies. Cultural-studies theorists focus instead on the qualities of the audience itself, it being, in their view, primarily an assemblage of individual producers of meaning.

The argument of proponents of an active audience rests on a reading of the social characteristics of what they consider underlie "late capitalism," which, as they see it, contains a large variety of social groups and subcultures. These either share in or contest the governance of the social order. In either case, it resolves into a restatement of the familiar pluralism perspective: no one group governs. The various social enclaves are structured along racial, ethnic, occupational, gender, age, and other lines. Each possesses its own history, experience, and, most important, specific interests. There is continuous change and shifts in the alignments.

A national or local audience today, according to this analysis, is an aggregation of many of these subgroupings. Of necessity, it must be a highly variegated population. Additionally, each individual in this audience works out her or his own meanings of the material being transmitted. The viewer, therefore, is actively producing meaning while consuming the media product or program. Indeed, the viewer's production of meaning, according to this now-dominant cultural theory, is no less important than, and it may surpass, that of the media producer. Thus, the relationship between the program producer—the employee of the corporate cultural conglomerate—and the individual meaning producer is at least roughly equal. Diversity, therefore, in this way of looking at television, does not require a variety of programmatic material. It is provided by the viewers in their capability to produce a diversity of readings or meanings in the single program.

Proponents of the active-audience view insist also on its liberating and subversive features. A great emphasis is given to the "resistance," "subversion," and "empowerment" of the viewer. Where this resistance and subversion of the audience lead and what effects they have on the existing structure of power remain a mystery. But there is no difficulty discovering what the practical effects of this theorizing are. The *New York Times,* for example, generously devoted half a page to a discussion of the doctoral thesis of a (then) Israeli graduate student, Tamar Liebes, who studied the impact of the popular TV program *Dallas* in Israel.[21]

The interest of the *Times*'s correspondent was piqued by the dissertation's point of inquiry and central hypothesis—"that foreign audiences are not merely blank slates upon which are etched the underlying message of American television programs." The project, it was further noted, "relates to a larger debate about the so-called [sic] American cultural imperialism—the extent to which American programs, art, culture, and other values are exported and overwhelm those of foreign countries."[22] Applying the active-audience frame of analysis, the study included four groups of Israeli viewers: Israeli Arabs, Moroccan Jewish immigrants, kibbutz members, and new Russian immigrants. The researcher found that the message that was imparted by *Dallas* depended on the viewer's values and varied according to the experiences of the particular group to which the viewer belonged. Accordingly, each group of viewers carried away a message that differed significantly from those received by viewers in the other three groups.

Assuredly, this was a finding most agreeable to the producers and one that sharply rebuffed the worriers who championed a new international information order. How heartening to the cultural message makers to learn that cultural imperialism does not exist! Each audience receives and makes its own message. Liebes concluded: "The idea of a simple 'American' message imposing itself in the same way on viewers all over the world is simply not valid."[23]

But who would have made such a claim in the first place? The transfer of cultural values is a complex matter. It is not a one-shot hypodermic innoculation of individual plots and character representations. It involves the much more difficult to measure acceptance of deep-structured meanings that may not even be explicitly stated. Can the transfer, for example, of acquisitive or consumerist perspectives be simply quantified?

Dallas, a seemingly world-popular TV program and thereby an irresistible subject for communication researchers, was the focus of another study by a University of Amsterdam academic Ien Ang. Whatever else the researcher had in mind, she found a strong need, as did Liebes, to confront what she termed "a stubborn fixation on the threat of 'American cultural imperialism.' "[24] Leaving aside the dubious methodology of Ang's study (inserting an ad in a magazine and asking readers to write to her about their reactions to viewing *Dallas;* forty-two letters "form the empirical material" of the analysis), the author found that the program's popularity came from the pleasure it provided the viewer. When asked why *Dallas* is pleasurable, the author informs us: "In order to answer such questions we should not inquire what are the social, economic and psychological characteristics of the public, but should rather ask ourselves what happens in the process of watching *Dallas.* It is in the actual confrontation between viewer and programme that pleasure is primarily generated."[25] With Ang as with others, the production of meaning is an individual act, in which the program/text is no more influential than what the viewer/reader makes of it. Power is equally distributed between the cultural producer and the consumer of the product.

In much the same manner, Robyn Penman, former president of the Australian Communication Association, insists on the primacy of the audience while dismissing the idea of mass-media power and of the influence of transnational corporations as major sources of message flow and cultural influence on national culture. "Individual citizens and nationwide audiences," she writes, "are, in fact, active participants in the communication process whether it be mass mediated or face-to-face." Her conclusion, therefore, is:

> Rather than imputing unsubstantiated communicative powers to the mass media and the multinational corporations we should be concerned with identifying the real and potential powers of the citizens who are also participants in the communication process.[26]

Another expression of this now popular, if not dominant, view found a hospitable outlet in *Daedalus,* the American establishment's (high) cultural organ. Along with insisting that meaning comes from the receiver, not the producer, of the message, Michael Tracy discounted the views of those who still cling to a belief that institutionalized cultural domination remains the basic condition of international and national communication. The last ten years, Tracy observed, have demonstrated a "greater emphasis on audience dispositions and intentions." Tracy's dating of the historical reemergence of the "limited-effects"–active-audience perspective corresponds nicely with the cresting of the movement for a new international information order in 1976 at Nairobi. This was the time, too, of the beginning of the U.S. counter-offensive against the New International Information Order, culminating in the U.S. withdrawal from UNESCO in 1984.

Tracy calls the model that confers primacy on the message maker a "deformed" paradigm. He argues that the principal task of communication research is "to enter into the different subjective meanings people create in popular movements, religion, journalism, everyday speech, and mass mediated events in order to interpret these meanings and bring them into a more systematic picture of the world view and ethos of a social order."[27]

Aggregating people's subjective meanings is a task that exceeds the capability of the most advanced supercomputers. Still, it manages to siphon away energy from the study of measurable sources and forms of power and influence. Tracy acknowledges this:

Those who favor the idea of cultural dominance through television have tended to study company reports, rather than the realities of human lives.[28]

Here again, the argument is reductionist. Cultural dominance does not derive from television imagery exclusively. TV is but one of a panoply of cultural means that *together* provide the apparatus of domination and the condition of dependency.

Reviewing essentially the same literature (Katz, Liebes, Ang, et al.), English sociologist Philip Schlesinger, cautions: " . . . the new revisionists' [active-audience theorists] position forces a breach between politico-economic arguments about the production of culture and the ways it is consumed and interpreted. However, although the pleasure of a text should not be underestimated, pleasure should not totally displace a concern with power." Schlesinger observes that in the works of the revisionists, "culture . . . shrinks in scope, and appears to be quite outside any relations of power or domination at all."[29]

The Western effort to stall and deflect the near-global movement for change in the prevailing international information-cultural order has received support from the active-audience explanation of cultural power. This theory has served to minimize, if not cast doubt on, the influence of concentrated media-cultural power.

The wide acceptance and the strength of the active-audience thesis reside partly in the theory's capacity to give pleasure to its formulators and believers; much more pleasure, perhaps, than they insist television programs give their viewers. This pleasure exists in the thesis's assurance that power rests with the viewer. How much more satisfying to be told that you already possess power than to be instructed that you must struggle for it against some very formidable opponents. One of the chief criticisms made against analysts who describe the power of the cultural industries is that their emphasis on the enormity of monopoly power is paralysing, defeatist, and, in any case, does not tell you what to do against it. Additionally, the complaint states that the changes that do occur in the products of the cultural industries are unaccounted for by a political economy analysis.

Those who complain that they become discouraged when apprised of the reality are signaling clearly that they do not want to do anything about that reality. With regard to the frequent representational changes that indisputably do appear in cultural-media outputs, it must be asked if these changes are the result of audience resistance and its efforts to make its own wishes felt.

The audience does count. But not in the way the active-audience theory explains. The managers of the cultural industries are acutely sensitive to the moods and feelings of the nation's many publics. It is their job, for which they are paid handsomely, to make day-by-day, if not hour-by-hour, assessments of these feelings. When they are mistaken, as they frequently are, they lose their jobs. But more significant than the sensitized antennae of the industrial-cultural decision makers, are the deep structural changes occurring in the economy and the social order itself. These produce new attitudes, anxieties, needs, and ambivalences in everyone. The pressures of a consumer society and the inequalities in the wage system that necessitate the two-job family, the extra strains imposed on women who are working and at the same time raising families, black and brown claims for larger shares in the resource pie, the hard-to-ignore effects of the destruction of the national and local environments, the threat of interventions in foreign locales, plant shutdowns and the fear of unemployment, two-tier employment, and a multitude of other socially unattended problems, all of them the outcome of market forces, affect individual lives in variable ways and with ferocious impact.

Why must the cultural industries take these issues into account? If they fail completely to do so and offer escapist programming exclusively, their ability to attract, hold, and involve an audience disappears. The audience, active or not, is on the receiving end of these social forces and the changes they are producing. Its perspectives cannot avoid being influenced by them. The cultural industries are compelled to tap into these new social situations, however they may misinterpret or distort them, if they hope to retain their connection with a population whose living arrangements are literally under siege.

Relatedly, the industries have at their disposal a very elaborate, expensive, and sophisticated technology—polling and surveying—to ascertain popular preferences, likes and dislikes, expectations, etc. Beyond its original applications to marketing and entertainment, it is used increasingly for a wide range of political and social functions, e.g., political candidates, campaigns, etc.

Another seeming strength of the active-audience hypothesis is its indisputable assertion that Western society, America in particular, is not a single homogeneous mass but an aggregate of innumerable groups and subgroups. Nothwithstanding this visible condition, the existence of a multitude of socially different groupings is hardly proof of either democratic governance of the state or diffusion of power in the society overall. Quite the contrary! Whatever the unique experiential history of each of the many subgroups in the nation, they are all subject to the rule of market forces and the domination of capital over those market forces. This is the grand common denominator that insures basic inequality in the social order, an inequality that the pluralists and the active-audience culturalists most often overlook.

In an earlier time, two of the more influential scholars whose work focuses on audience response paid close attention in their writing to this fundamental feature of the social landscape. John Fiske and John Hartley pointed out in 1978 how television, for example, blurs the omnipresent class division in Western society. TV programs, they noted, *always* encode (carry) the message of the dominant class. Though the dominated class may be offered a program menu that features the affluence and the glitter of the privileged elite, in the end, "the class condition at the connotative level usually emerges as like-us subordinate."[30] The ultimate message in TV, then, is that the dominating class has the same basic problems as the dominated and is itself not in control of its destiny. Further:

> . . . In the world of television, division between classes *in themselves* are rarely if ever presented as such. Television articulates the responses of people to their class condition, not the class condition itself. Hence it is primarily a medium for the expression of *classes for themselves*. Here again, however, the expression is rarely one of oppositional solidarity of

either the dominant or the subordinate class to one another. Rather television—along with most other commercial enterprises—exploits the competitive fragmentation among people who belong to what is objectively, the same, subordinate class. Hence social divisions on television as elsewhere emerge as a kind of sliding scale of social stratification as opposed to primary class division.[31]

Well put! Yet in similar kinds of analyses ten years later, consideration of class is conspicuously absent. Could it be that such an emphasis might be a depressant to the "pleasure-seeking" viewer who now occupies the attention of current theoretical work?

Less significant, but not without interest, is another characteristic frequently present in some of the work of the active-audience writers—the confessional statement. It is supposed to disarm skeptics by providing a personal testimonial by someone who, we should obviously recognize, has proven credentials of unorthodoxy. By no means atypical, Elayne Rapping (who generally has many interesting things to say about the media industries and their products) feels obliged to inform her readers that "As a viewer, for example, I like to watch soap opera. My daughter and I love to discuss the latest goings on of Brook English, Tad Martin, and the other residents of Pine Valley, a town we often escape to when we're both home."[32] Other writers recall nostalgically how they enjoyed this or that program when they were children. This is done apparently to assure the reader that *they* survived and developed a critical consciousness. You can take your pleasure and you will not be permanently damaged is the subtextual point they are making.

The Biggest Blind Spot of All

Beyond the theoretical objections to the active-audience thesis—its dismissal of class, its overly optimistic attribution of social pluralism, its excessive subjectivity—recent information management over the entire media spectrum in the United States calls into question the very possibility of audience participation in, much less resistance to, the messages transmitted. In these messages there is no room for interpretation and transformative potential. What can be said, for example, about the shadowy but many-tentacled disinformation industry— actually an integral part of the cultural industries, orchestrated by the political elite and the intelligence agencies since the end of World War II? Arabs (and Quadafi and Arafat in particular), the Sandinistas,

Castro, and other perceived adversaries of U.S. power have been at one time or another the targets of the disinformation apparatus.

One of its main messages for nearly half a century has been anticommunism—whether filling the news bulletins, inserted in the plots of television dramas and countless Hollywood films, or the multimillion-copy Cold War spy novel (which is at the top of the best-seller list month in and month out). J. Fred MacDonald, analyst of popular culture, documented the massive flow of anticommunist material which passed through television channels in the twenty years from the end of World War II through the intervention in Vietnam. It is a record of an intensive, uniform, and undeviating conditioning of the American mind with the anticommunist message, differing only in format and crudity. MacDonald demonstrates that TV's early owners (Paley, Sarnoff, et al.) and its prominent personalities of the period (Cronkhite, Huntley, Smith, Swayze, etc.), with rare exceptions, were cosily collaborating with the Pentagon, the FBI, The Voice of America, and other state organs of persuasion and coercion. Commercial television had no problems making and peddling the narratives and visuals of the Cold War line to the American people. Just as assiduously, TV's controllers purged their domain of writers, performers, and staff who were accused of not conforming to the standards that were demanded by the right-wing crusaders of that time.[33]

A question for those who write so confidently about audience "resistance" is, "Where, except for a saving few, has there been a public outcry against the enormous fabrication of fear that has supported the edifice of the national security state for at least fifty years?" Consider the admission of William Attwood, who traveled alongside, if not *in,* the highest ranks of the policymakers, that the Cold War was an illusion—really a deception—that "Moscow conspired to take over Western Europe by force."[34] The assessment of Alan Tonelson, Twentieth-Century Fund author, is the same: "Even during Western Europe's darkest days, it is now clear that few important American officials expected the Soviet assault that they warned of to muster domestic support for the Marshall Plan and NATO."[35]

All of the dreadful policies that have followed from that false prospect—forty years of arms build-up for "national security"; the creation of NATO and the remilitarization of Germany and Japan (the latter is still being handled discreetly); the numerous U.S. military interventions around the world to forestall Soviet "aggression"; the attack on American civil liberties at home—were based on a lie, a lie foisted on the public with dismaying success, with the full and indispensable complicity of the cultural industries. It is not a matter of people being dupes, informational or cultural. It is that human beings are not equipped to deal with a pervasive disinformational system—administered from the commandposts of the social order—that assaults the senses through all cultural forms and channels.

Audiences do, in fact, interpret messages variously. They also may transform them to correspond with their individual experiences and tastes. But when they are confronted with a message incessantly repeated in all cultural conduits, issuing from the commanders of the social order, their capacities are overwhelmed. People also respond when breakdowns occur—that is, ruptures in the control process. But this happens after the fact. Can the response be made *before* the crisis erupts? This may be the decisive question in the time ahead.

In the late 1980s, the control of representation and definition remains concentrated in the products and services of media-cultural combines. That control can be challenged and lessened only by political means. Theories that ignore the structure and locus of representational and definitional power and emphasize instead the individual's message transformational capability present little threat to the maintenance of the established order.

| 8 |

Public Expression in a Crisis Economy

The corporate envelopment of public expression and creativity has been a direct outgrowth of the enormous expansion of corporate wealth and power in the postwar decades. The centrality of the corporation in the U.S. economy was evident as well in the spheres of information, public expression, and culture. The industrial ascendancy of America was matched by its global domination of information and media flows.

Though many of these features linger, the era of the American century has come and gone. This is still to be fully understood by the public at large. The new second-class condition gets only piecemeal acknowledgement. The extent of the historical realignment is blurred by blustering bravado of the national political leadership. There is also, more consequentially, the continued presence if not growth of the nuclear stockpile. The country is turning, therefore, in the words of one pragmatic observer, "into a historical anomaly . . . a first-rate military power and a second-rate economic power."[1] The changes have come so rapidly that the American predicament is seen often as comparable to the problems afflicting an individual. In this sense, it could be said that the American market economy is facing an "identity crisis."

At first, the country's intellectuals had convinced themselves and others that since the 1960s we were living in a postindustrial society. Accordingly, the problems associated with industrial capitalism, not least the divisions between social classes, were no longer applicable and certainly not worth worrying over. Those who continued to concern themselves with such matters gave evidence, according to the new thinking, of their own obsolescence.

There were more metamorphoses to come. The postindustrial society became a "services economy," soon thereafter to be replaced by an "information society." Now, a reappraisal of sorts seems to be in the making. In 1987, attention was given to those who proclaimed, "manufacturing matters."[2] There is some basis for this active semantic shuffling. There have been transformations in the production process. Automation and other efficiency measures have increased industrial output while allowing the work force to be reduced. Labor *is* increasingly employed in nonmanufacturing and nonagricultural jobs, most of which can be regarded as service-connected. The United States, Western Europe, and especially Japan have recently had a great expansion in financial and property-related transactional services. Banking, real estate, insurance, media, and recreational activities have responded vigorously to the general growth in the capitalist system and its internationalization.

These substantial and visible changes notwithstanding, the underlying mechanisms of the economic order—its fundamental dynamics—remain intact. There is still a working class, engaged though it may be in different kinds of jobs. There is still an owning class with a dominant stake in new as well as older forms of enterprise. The working class continues to be separated from the productive machinery, whether it be industrial plants or computational installations or media facilities. The owning class still enjoys the private appropriation of the economy's surplus, however it may be generated.

Another fundamental characteristic of capitalism has not disappeared, regardless of what the system is presently called. Cyclical crises remain a recurrent feature. "Glutted markets" and "global overcapacity" once again are topical.[3] "All over the globe, in developed and developing nations alike," a business correspondent reports, "producers in a broad spectrum of industries are turning out more than consumers can buy, creating a new world economy—a glut economy."[4]

Whether the United States has a postindustrial service or information economy, it unmistakeably has a "glut economy." Given the unfilled elemental needs of a large part of the American population, to say nothing of the desperate human condition of at least half of humanity, the idea of "glut" is grotesque if not obscene. However, in the prevailing economic order, its existence is a reminder that profit, not need, continues to be the determinant of economic activity. Capitalism, by this measure, definitely has not evolved into a new stage.

Yet for a quarter of a century, preceding the revival of interna-

tional industrial competition, cyclical gyrations and hard-nosed managerial responses to threats of market loss were absent. The U.S.
economy was at the center of the world economic order, profiting
from and expanding because of its privileged position. Contributing
further to what at the time seemed like a new age were the economic
stimuli provided by the military interventions in Korea and Vietnam.

Great as they were, these military expenditures were dwarfed by
the outlays in the Reagan years. In this period, the expenditures
deepened rather than alleviated the unfolding economic crisis. In the
earlier period, however, the corporate sector had flourished and extended its influence across the social landscape. Will the late 1980s
and after, probably a time of intensifying pressure from the many
serious and unattended systemic problems, see a reduction of corporate power and influence? Will the besieged economic sphere be
accompanied with cutbacks all along the line?

One national experience not to repeat but to reflect on is the Great
Depression of the 1930s. The costs in human suffering were great,
and the shock produced by the industrial collapse was profound. The
long-dominant ideology of private enterprise and its many myths that
had governed individual behavior for generations were not credible in
those years. The business system and its values also lost authority.
Confidence in the market as an efficient regulator of national economic activity disappeared. The issue no longer was whether there
should be state intervention. How far intervention should go was the
question given political attention. There were many who felt that the
private-enterprise model was beyond repair. Whatever the opinion,
the political arena was active and the range of debate, at least by the
standards of recent years, incredibly wide.

The arts, too, displayed enormous energy and critical ferment.
Establishment control over social expression was loosened. Public
works were constructed. Plays were financially underwritten with public funds, staged excitingly, and captured new audiences. Novels with
social themes poured forth. Murals were painted in public buildings.
Guidebooks were produced that detailed the many sites and voices of
a noncorporate America.

In the creative work of the '30s, individualism, aestheticism, elit-
ism, art for art's sake were hardly absent, but they did not dominate
the field. Social concerns infused content. The works produced were
meaningful to those who encountered them. Not unexpectedly, the
creative work of the '30s was downgraded, if not largely rejected, in
the postwar years of renascent corporate power and growth. The new

arbiters of taste, beneficiaries of the (short) global reign of American influence, had little enthusiasm for the social views and outlooks that marked the slump decade.

In the 1990s, a revival of critical political expression in the space that may be created by the economy's weakness and decline is not out of the question. It is also not very likely. The economic order has changed structurally in the last fifty years. The character and salient features of the postwar system point to other cultural, political, and economic outcomes. The chief difference today between the contemporary economic order and its prewar condition is the pervasive internationalization of capital. This is coincidental with an enormously increased command of resources and financial assets. The dominant corporations now are transnational in their operations and their physical locales. The leading companies (industrial and service) carry on their business in dozens of countries. IBM, for example, is active in more than 100 countries.

This means that the main economic actors in the American economy—the biggest employers, the largest producers, the heaviest advertisers—are not nearly as focused on the national market as they were in the prewar years. In some fields, U.S. companies derive more than half of their revenues and profits from sales outside the home territory. In most instances, the foreign returns exceed 25 percent.

The transnational corporate sector of the American economy, its dominant component, now responds to the international economic environment. This diminishes, at least somewhat, the strategic importance of the home market. A key advantage of the new international order is the opportunity it offers its leading players, the transnational corporations, to escape national pressure from the state labor or resource availabilities. Activity now is relatively easily transferred from one international site to another. How effective this transferability factor would be in a time of severe international crisis is yet to be seen. Clearly, the interactivity that now characterizes international economic transactions could as easily intensify as well as lessen disequilibrating stimuli.

Still, in the more limited situation of *national* economic difficulty, the transnational companies have managed quite well to date. So well, in fact, that they have succeeded in escaping various strains by transferring them to the national economy. The country's distressing international trade deficit, for example, is largely attributable to the big transnational companies who have shifted operations to cheaper locations outside the continental boundaries.

The question of concern is whether a repetition of the 1930s type of economic crisis can be expected. If it can, will it allow the social space that opened up then to reappear and sustain the revival of political challenge and extended social criticism? Much depends on the behavior of the state. What will be its stance toward a transnational corporate order that is contributing to national disequilbrium? Heavily influenced by that order, can the American state exercise sufficient autonomous authority to override its strongest constituents?

The strong state, as a regulating instrument of potential economic crisis and political disorder, has powerful friends and defenders, some of whom are in the transnational corporate community itself. It may be recalled that the presiding chief justice of the Supreme Court has indicated more than once his willingness to accept the authority of the state over the interests of the transnational corporation.

There are other advocates as well of the idea and practice of the strong state. Elements of the business sector, for example, that are not so heavily transnationalized look to government for protection of their share of the domestic market against foreign suppliers. The transnationals themselves are not beyond calling on the state to rein in their foreign rivals.

More weighty still are the constitutive elements of the strong state. Built up and reinforced throughout the twentieth century, these agencies of the state are in a position to influence heavily their own futures. This is especially evident, but by no means an exceptional instance, with respect to the American military establishment. Recipient of more than a trillion dollars of public funds in the last five years, the military touches the livelihood of people across the nation, reaching into the smallest communities. Cuts in military appropriations, therefore, are not only resisted by generals and admirals and defense contractors. Large numbers of working people, fearful of job loss and unconvinced that compensatory public expenditures will keep them at work, make up a powerful political support group for the strong state.

Besides the military expansion, police, investigatory, and intelligence functions have grown considerably in recent decades. These, too, constitute important pillars of the strong state. From time to time, some egregious intrusion by one or another of these agencies' representatives into citizens' lives, receives brief publicity. The (usually) illegal acts are then represented as aberrations, some individual transgressions contrary to the agencies' rules, practices, and ethical standards. Often, the only exceptionality of the acts resides in discovery and the public attention devoted to them. The behavior of the Federal Bureau of Investigation (FBI), for example, since the time of its establishment in the post-World I years (a time span of seventy years) is a record of repeated violations of citizens' democratic rights.[5] The motivation for these actions—with just enough exceptions for the Bureau to argue it is even-handed—has been the harassment and intimidation of radicals, civil-rights people, civil libertarians, and antiwar activists.

There is also a strong connection between the coercive practices of the "law and order" state organs and times of unsettlement and crisis. During the anti-Vietnamese War demonstrations in the late 1960s, for example, police and intelligence agencies were busy spying and provoking disturbances. For more than a hundred years, whenever there have been active periods of labor mobilization and demands, the police agencies invariably have discovered "reds" and "foreign agents."

After World War II, it was helpful to the ends of the aggressively expansionist American foreign policy to focus attention on the alleged "subversive" activities of domestic radicals. The Department of Justice prosecuted the leadership of the Communist party for "conspiracy to teach" the overthrow of the government by force and violence. "Conspiracy to teach" in that era of fabricated political emotionalism was sufficient charge for juries to convict and for federal justices to impose jail sentences on the leaders of a political party.

The Strong State in the Probable Crisis Years Ahead

Though not at all improbable in the light of historical experience, it is not a foregone conclusion that the strong state will come down hard on critical public expression in the all-too-likely crisis time ahead. It is still instructive to remember the historical record. The installation of fascist regimes in Italy and Germany and the deep inroads of fascist thinking and organization in France and England in the pre-World War II days cannot be forgotten. The record bears witness to the susceptibility of major stakeholders in industrial market economies to adopt ultrarepressive political regimes to protect their threatened positions in time of deep and protracted crises.

But it is also a fact that in the same era and under relatively similar circumstances of serious economic slump the dominant political forces in the United States opted for the New Deal and social reform. From this experience however, there is no assurance that the corporate governors in America are innoculated against the fascist (strong state) solution to a politically threatening crisis. The evidence in the preceding chapters emphasizes the erosion of democratic principle and practice in the informational-cultural sphere. Given this weakening of the national democratic fabric, the advent of the coercive state is hardly precluded.

Still, the corporate enclosure of cultural space, however extensive in the last fifty years, has not been total. There remain a number of centers of democratic and public expression, though they may be small-scale and geographically dispersed. Besides, as historical experience demonstrates, availability of overwhelming power does not guarantee its effective use or its use at all.

Restraints on the coercive state's power in recent years are demonstrable. The absence of an American military intervention in Central America, for example, cannot be explained by any factor other than popular opposition, even if only indirectly expressed. Another example has been the inability of the Reagan administration, despite its original intention, to cut social security benefits. The popular will on this has been unmistakeable. In situation after situation, the determining factor is the population's understanding of an issue and its ability to connect a proposed policy to self-interest. In the instance of a possible military invasion of some distant land, the personal or family cost is fully perceived. So, too, a proposal to slash social security benefits cannot conceal the impact upon millions of beneficiaries of the prevailing system.

But these are recognizable relationships. In many, if not most, of the urgent questions now surfacing, the personal connection may not be as readily apparent. This explains why the control of the mass media and the general informational system has become a key element either in maintaining or changing the status quo. How the media treat or ignore a problem constitutes a critical exercise of power.

Who will have determination in the exercise of that power? How will that power be used to define, explain, and even identify what the issues are? These have always been matters of the greatest relevance to the question of social control. In the information-using society, they are more important than ever. Accordingly, to accept the view that the informational system is neutral, merely a transmission apparatus, magnifies the problem. To imagine that the system is autonomous adds to the confusion.

This is why the subject of corporate speech, recently given legitimation, is of no small consequence to everyday life. If left unchallenged, the opportunity to create an expanded universe of public expression is almost foreclosed. More threatening still, the ease by which a strong state, using legal means, could further damage what remains of public expression is facilitated.

Theorizing over media influence, which puts determination and control in the hands of the individual viewer or listener or reader, gives critical, if unintended, support to the legitimacy of corporate speech. To the extent that attention is directed away from the message producer to the message receiver, the full significance of bestowing constitutional rights on corporate speech is hidden. If viewers actually are able to make up their own meanings and interpretations of messages, of what concern is the corporate voice, booming through and over the cultural landscape?

It cannot be overstated. The informational question, in all its dimensions—practical and theoretical—is an urgent political issue in America. Yet the national informational condition—what is seen, heard, and read—is worsening steadily. The central dilemma is that we are reliant on the information system to alert us to any malfunction in the system itself; but the apparatus has been shockingly, though not surprisingly, reticent in calling attention to its own ills.

The causes of the deepening information malady may be found in developments and trends in America's media and cultural industries: billion-dollar acquisitions in publishing; buyouts and takeovers of national television networks; growing oligopoly in cable TV; and the fulfillment of an advertiser's dream, the spread of the one-newspaper city. The United States now has what Ben Bagdikian, the former dean of the Graduate School of Journalism at the University of California, Berkeley, calls a "private ministry of information and culture."[6] The seeming pluralism provided by thousands of newspapers, magazines, radio stations, and TV channels is belied by their near-total absorption into giant media combines. The consequence is a national discourse that is increasingly one-dimensional. And although concentration in industry is as American as apple pie, its presence and metastic growth in the information-cultural field calls into question the elemental assumptions of democratic government. Can we be confident that the large institutions that preside over the society's daily output and intake of imagery and information are adequately informing the citizenry?

In addition to the enfeeblement of the public's access to information is the heavy utilization of the new data/communications technologies for commercial ends. The emerging capabilities for organizing, processing, storing, retrieving, and disseminating information have encouraged the entry of private firms into the information business.

The commercialization of information, its private acquisition and sale, has become a major industry. While more material than ever before, in formats created for specialized use, is available at a price, free public information supported by general taxation is attacked by the private sector (and its friends inside the national government) as an unacceptable form of subsidy.

Responding to its business clientele, the Reagan-era team tried, in effect, to eliminate the public information sector. It staffed executive and regulatory agencies, the Office of Management and Budget and the Federal Communications Commission in particular, with trusted stewards whose mission was to speed up privatization and commercialization of as many government functions as possible. "Ability to pay" has become, thereby, the governing principle of access to information.

Prerequisites for Challenging the Information-Cultural Complex

Changing the informational-media national condition beyond cosmetic improvements does not represent just another instance of a single-issue political effort. The democratization of the informational order, its disengagement from an all-encompassing corporate connection, and ventilation of genuinely alternative social visions collide directly with the underpinnings of power in the economy at large. Florida's forced submission to corporate media power when its state legislature attempted to impose a tax on advertising is no isolated or exceptional episode.

The information-cultural component has become integral to the maintenance of corporate economic activity worldwide, to political mastery at home and abroad, and to social control in general. System-wide alarm signals go off quickly when the informational sphere is even mildly questioned. A recent instance of this was the publication of a *draft* letter of reflections on the U.S. economy by the American Catholic bishops. They wrote:

> . . . We believe that the level of inequality in income and wealth in our society and even more the inequality on the world scale today must be judged morally unacceptable. The fulfillment of the basic needs of the poor is of the highest priority.

The bishops concluded that the stimulation of consumer demand in the United States presented serious moral and economic problems. In their view, "A consumerist mentality which encourages immediate gratification mortgages our future and ultimately risks undermining the foundations of a just order."[7] These sentiments, *if acted upon,* would imperil the foundations of the entire corporate economy. Immediately at risk would be the key mechanisms in the market economy—the stimulation of consumer demand by advertising and the ideology of freedom. (Freedom is interpreted as the opportunity to choose between different automobile models or soap products.)

Aware of the danger of allowing such views to pass unchallenged, days *before* the draft letter was formally released, a private group of eminent Catholics, highly placed in the corporate and government worlds, did its best to defuse the bishops' imminent letter of criticisms of the economy. The private group's statement (written and endorsed by such luminaries as William E. Simon, former secretary of the treasury; Alexander M. Haig, former secretary of state; and J. Peter Grace of W. R. Grace & Co. and chair of the President's Commission on Privatization) was a eulogy of private enterprise: "As democratic capitalism has developed in the United States, the economic system responds to the legitimate demands of the political system, including those who, for whatever reason, are not working and need assistance."[8] Yet it is precisely the refusal of the system to respond to these legitimate demands that constitutes the main point of criticism of the bishops' letter. But no matter! The objective of the private Catholic group was to undercut the bishops' statement.

The instantaneous opposition of powerful groups to views that question central systemic functioning is to be expected. In fact, it is an acknowledgment that the seat of power has been identified and called to account. It is of the greatest importance, therefore, to persist in making the systemic links of the informational-cultural complex widely known and understandable to as many as possible.

The Ideological Bases of the Information-Cultural Complex

The strength of the prevailing information-media complex rests on its command of vast material assets and the near-universal acceptance of its own definition and description of its role and function. It is the ideological strength that requires analysis and reappraisal. As good as any place to begin is with the concept of a "free press," the generally unquestioned premise of the information order.

Can the prevailing belief that private ownership is synonymous with and guarantor of a free press be taken for granted? Assuredly, the press will not question this proposition. It is their bedrock defense. It is also the hammer with which the media establishment pounds away at alternate press institutions in other countries, socialist *or* capitalist. According to the free-press catechism, it is private ownership and private financing—advertising—that provide the bases of freedom. Support coming out of state revenues—ultimately derived from the population—is regarded as tainted and potentially tyrannical.

In quoting or referring to reporting emanating from nonmarket economies, the U.S. media not infrequently preface the account with a warning—similar to the cautionary words on a cigarette package—that the information comes from a "state-controlled" press. Would it not be equally appropriate to preface domestic reporting with the indisputable point that it customarily comes from privately owned billion-dollar companies?

Although a certain amount of popular skepticism and unease do exist, the trust that the private informational system has been able to create, maintain, and insulate itself with is remarkable. Rarely is there a murmur from any influential quarter that the information lifeline of the country is totally in the hands of vast, private, unaccountable domains. Criticism from the nonmedia sector of the corporate economy does occur, but it serves generally to further solidify the already dominant ideology that is disseminated. Any politician, incumbent or candidate, who might question the national information structure faces an instantaneous media backlash. The intellectual community, inside and outside academia, generally regard developments in the media as not worthy of intellectual consideration.

Where does this leave us? First, on the positive side, there are thousands of experienced and skilled media people in the country working to provide alternative modes of expression. They produce programming for local cable-access channels. They edit and publish small independent papers and magazines and even some books. They unfailingly critique the dominant media. There are also significant numbers of individuals in the commercial media, constrained by their limits, but attempting nevertheless to undertake and carry out projects that may add something to human enlightenment and well-being.

The independents, the alternative media workers and the conscientious commercial-media employees, constitute an important national cultural-informational resource. Under different conditions, they could easily produce an alternate diet of informational and recreational programming for national and local publics. It is hard to see, however, their endeavors *by themselves* changing significantly the contours and content of the dominant U.S. informational system. It is instructive to cite as evidence of the possible influence of independent message-making the tapes and programming, for example, that contributed to the Iranian Revolution. The messages of the then-exiled Ayatollah Khomeini were disseminated by alternative means, it is true. But the crucial ingredient present in Iran then and lacking at this time in the United States is a receptive, *organized* audience, willing to act upon the message transmitted.

The messages of the independents and the alternative-media producers in the United States (even when they are circulated—though most often they reach only a small audience) do not generate great popular appeal. The American audience remains encapsulated in a corporate-message cocoon. It is very unlikely that this cocoon will be removed by the efforts of a still-miniscule noncommercial media community, admirable as it is.

A similar conclusion must be drawn about the high expectations for the creation of alternative informational networks by those using their personal computers. Such networks already exist and may grow denser and stronger. Yet they are insignificant when compared with the tremendous computational power at the disposal of the major power clusters of the country—the Pentagon, the intelligence agencies, the police, the big corporations, etc. This is not to disparage the efforts of those who are striving to create new and more responsive informational systems. The objective here is to assess the likelihood of these new arrangements making a fundamental difference in what now exists. By that criterion, judgment on individual computing activities must remain skeptical.

It is hardly revelatory, therefore, to conclude that making a difference that counts in the informational-cultural situation depends on political action. It means that the issues that have been considered in these pages must become high-priority items in the agenda of a socially oriented political movement. It also suggests that such a movement has to meet head-on the all-too-likely storm of opposition and opprobrium it will quickly and inevitably encounter. The now dominant corporate informational sector will not take kindly to a reform movement that questions seriously its structure and practices.

From this conclusion, it may seem that the information-cultural question is in a state of indefinite limbo. But this leaves out of the equation the larger context, the contemporary American political scene, to say nothing of the international picture. The crisis conditions facing the American economy in the post-Reagan era cannot fail to activate intense political reactions and personal involvements. The long-standing acceptance of labor-capital mutuality, never total to be sure, along with the tweedle-dum-tweedle-dee politics of the postwar period may be coming to an end. Far-reaching economic decisions cannot be deferred indefinitely. Harsh reallocation of national resources will have to be effected—one way or another. Different groups will benefit or suffer, depending on how the resource choices are made. Given the seemingly inescapable economic crunch ahead, the revival of political interest and activism is a near certainty. Political polarization and social-class conflict (viewed in recent years as obsolete concepts) are no less likely.

A brief word about the international scene also is in order. Some very obvious fault lines of future upheaval are very close to the surface and easily visible to those who are not willfully blind. The last twenty years have seen a parade of cheap victories over movements for national sovereignty around the world: Western reluctance either to assist economically weak societies or to permit them to make their own independent decisions has prevailed. But no longlasting stability has been achieved.

The costs of patrolling and controlling the poor world escalate. Removing the visible signs of discontent from popular view are temporary expedients. Shutting off the TV cameras on the West Bank, in Soweto, and elsewhere does not change the reality. Eruption of one or several of these centers of oppression and exploitation in the near future is inevitable. Resort to the customary measures to subdue such outbreaks can only place heavier strains on the already burdened American economy.

Immediately after the Second World War, in a situation of imperial crisis, Britain was forced to yield its commanding position in one possession or sphere of influence after another. In almost every case (Greece was an early example), the United States substituted itself for the former governing power. Who or what will fill in for declining American global power? And will that already observable decline be accelerated by such pressure from the formerly dependent regions? How these developments play themselves out constitutes another considerable, but immeasurable, factor affecting the domestic sociocultural scene in the years ahead.

An Agenda for the Future

How will these different pressures, domestic and international, be experienced by Americans? First and foremost, it already is and will increasingly be matters of jobs and living standards. The present controllers of the economy will act as they have in the past. In times of crisis, when there are sacrifices to be made, they will try to impose the burdens on those least capable of resisting them—the poor, the weak, the lower-income groups. Such, for example, would be the effect of an increased sales tax, introduced to meet the increasingly urgent need to raise federal revenues. Whatever the specific means employed to overcome the grievous economic imbalances that have been built up over the years, the central issue will be: *who must sacrifice?*

The media-informational aspect of the looming domestic crisis bears a striking ressemblance to that which faced the newly independent nations in the postwar years. In their case, the achievement of political independence, though long-sought and warmly welcomed, was quickly seen to be insufficient. Economic independence was also necessary. When efforts turned to gaining economic breathing space, still another vital ingredient of independence was found to be missing. This was cultural-informational autonomy. Independent economic development, it was discovered by some, could not be attained as long as the informational system pumped in messages and imagery from the outside. These established the models in people's minds of what "development" should look like. Thus was born the movement for a New International Information Order (NIIO). That objective has not been realized. In most of the poor countries of Africa, Asia, and Latin America, dependent development and dependent culture continue to prevail.

This has its lesson, ironically enough, for the people in the United States. In the crisis years ahead, unless the informational-cultural sector is a priority field for attention, the possibility of effecting *other* changes in the economy that meet the basic needs of the majority of the population will be greatly diminished, if realizable at all. Can one imagine, for instance, the corporate media explaining to its audiences why a sales tax is inequitable and falls most heavily on those with the lowest incomes or (not so unlikely) media presentations demonstrating why transnational corporations should have tax breaks—the argument being that these will provide more capital for investment—while their work force should be required to offer "give-backs"? How will the advertiser-supported TV and press explain the need for "general austerity" while promoting daily appeals to buy this or consume that?

How can public xenophobia and chauvinism be avoided when the role of American-owned transnational companies in the world economy remains a mystery to everyone? A black hole of ignorance about transnational corporate activity is the outcome of systematic omission of information and its meaningful analysis. And, directly related, how can the xenophobic attitudes that arise from this ignorance be countered in an informational and political system that *uses* these impulses to divert attention from the actual sources of the national troubles? In this sense, the U.S. informational-cultural condition is similar to that in the dominated excolonial countries. In both, the control of the messages and imagery prevent an objective assessment of reality. They contribute instead to misconceptions that lend support to policies that benefit the few to the great disadvantage of the many.

The post-Reagan period will be a time of diminishing American international influence and, more than likely, economic contraction at home. In this strained environment, a new information-cultural direction has to be a core component of whatever political movement for new national goals develops. A hundred years ago, for example, the public demanded antitrust legislation to protect it against the monopoly practices of railroads, grain millers, and the big banks. A different type of regulation may be required today, but the need to safeguard thought and consciousness against private informational monopoly is just as urgent.

A political movement that takes up the information issue will be accused almost at once of seeking information management and of trespassing on the First Amendment. The answer to that charge is straightforward. The national information system is managed already. The point of the debate and the program for change is to move the locus of the existing political and economic control of information from private corporate decision-making to public participation and accountability. A full-scale review of the country's informational-cultural situation is long overdue. It grows increasingly urgent.

A modest step in this direction is the support of the Association of American Universities of a report by John Shattuck and Muriel Morisey Spence, two Harvard researchers, recommending the reversal of the information policies adopted or strengthened in the Reagan era.[9] The report calls upon the newly elected president, Mr. Bush, in January 1989 to overhaul current governmental information policies. It claims that "information policies pursued by the federal government over the past decade have had a significant negative impact on important aspects of national life . . . Important values of free speech, academic inquiry, and democratic participation have all been adversely affected by the recent trends in federal information policy." To overcome these perilous trends the report suggests that "within the first 100 days the new administration should signal a shift in policy by issuing an executive order revising the classification and export control systems [applied to information]." Additionally, it urges that the federal information-management authority of the Office of Management and Budget (OMB) be sharply curtailed and its policy of turning over federal information functions to the private sector be halted. It proposes that Mr. Bush deliver a message to the Congress advocating a federal information policy in full accord with the First Amendment, grounded on the principles of free and open communication.

This would be a beginning. In a full-scale effort to restore public participation and accountability to media and cultural affairs, a 180-degree shift in the policy that has prevailed since the end of World War II and carried to its extreme in the Reagan years is the first order of business. This translates at the outset into a massive expansion of the public sector, the site which has suffered a severe contraction in recent years. The international as well as the domestic public sectors are involved.

Internationally, the persistent U.S. government attacks on the United Nations and its educational-scientific-cultural organization (UNESCO) deserve immediate repudiation. For years, the federal government has withheld a portion of its dues, severely obstructing the UN's activities. Additionally, the United States withdrew from UNESCO in 1984. Past dues should be paid in full, re-entry into UNESCO effected, and the proper respect to international efforts that seek cultural and informational sovereignty given.

It is understood that the beneficiaries of American information policy over the last half century—the media conglomerates and the transnational companies—will not be pleased with these changes. Their displeasure will be intensified if, in addition, their long-standing principle, "the free flow of information," is given a new and more democratic interpretation. A new version of "the free-flow" doctrine would aim at reducing private monopoly power over news, TV programs, films, music, data processing, publishing, and advertising. It would encourage the availability, as much as possible, of information as a social and inexpensive good, not, as increasingly the situation, as a salable commodity.

A new informational-cultural politics would have other basic features. It would signify the acceptance and vastly expanded public support and encouragement of noncommercial expression and creativity. Publicly financed newspapers, magazines, television, radio, theater, and film would become a legitimate part of the national social landscape. At the same time, this would be accompanied by a variety of managerial and administrative modes that would be intended to insulate these activities from the direction of the state. There is a wide repertory of experience and practice to be drawn on here. The important consideration is to allow for imaginative alternatives. Currently, the fashion is to deny that possibility.

The expansion of publicly supported facilities for information and creative expression, if undertaken, will almost automatically confer a new and richer meaning on the idea of the free flow of information. It would then, in fact, become a deeper and freer current of messages and imagery. And to the extent that this is realized, the concerns of the proponents for a new international information order would be satisfied. Diversity would replace homogeneity. The prevailing envelopment of American cultural space by the corporate presence also would be lessened. With fresh outputs originating in noncommercial centers of expression and creativity, the one-dimensional cultural scene would be expanded. The privilege now conferred on corporate speech no longer would be as worrisome; amplified public speech would see to that.

Still another feature of a new media-cultural politics would be the dethronement of technology. This does not mean its abandonment. The computer is here to stay—so are communication satellites and cable TV. They will continue to be important instruments for information dissemination and expression. What is intended by dethroning technology is to distinguish between using instrumentation for social ends and, as in current practice, using technology as a social end in itself. Indicative of the end-in-itself approach is the notion that because cable TV provides numerous channels the viewer's freedom is substantially enhanced. Yet there is no reason to be confident that this is the case. More likely under present corporate arrangements, a narrow range of familiar materials are transmitted regardless of the channel capacity.

Satellite communication also has been hailed as the answer to the needs of even the remotest of settlements, making available to many the holdings of the world's libraries, museums, and other repositories of the world's social knowledge and creations. Perhaps. To date, however, satellite communication has been utilized mostly for the data transmissions of transnational corporations and advertiser-supported sports spectaculars which bring the consumerist message into households around the world.

A truly new politics of information and culture, therefore, will put less emphasis on substituting modern instrumentation of communication for human organization, face-to-face meetings, and local and individual expression. Compared with computerized mailings, telephone solicitations, photo opportunities, political commercials, these human interactional modes may seem hopelessly out of date. Yet the "modern" methods really have nothing to do with establishing genuine popular support, independent thought, and political autonomy. They are the methodologies and technologies developed for corporate mass marketing and political manipulation.

The Drift of Events

Postwar developments in the informational-cultural sector at home and abroad do not give much encouragement to expectations for an expanded public sector of communication and cultural expression. The direction has been overwhelmingly the other way—away from the public and toward the private control of telecommunications, media, and cultural institutions. All the same, the dynamism of the corporate thrust cannot be maintained indefinitely—the world, in corporate terms, is a finite market. So, too, the instabilities and potential rupture points in the world economy overall have multiplied greatly in recent years.

In the wake of the stock-market collapse in October 1987, a dramatic, if short-lived, change was observable in the *New York Times*, the flagship organ of the Eastern establishment. On November 1, 1987, probably for the first time in forty years, that newspaper opened its columns, very sparingly to be sure, to views it customarily eschews. Commentators from varied radical currents, socialist and communist, were permitted, indeed solicited, to air their views about the market crash.[10] If a 500-point drop in share values could achieve this opening, what might a real and protracted slump do to the privatization policies that have prevailed so long?

Whether the opportunity appears to create a new political movement that will press to change the underlying economy in a significant way and whether that movement will take up seriously the media-cultural issue are beyond prediction. What can be said is this. The possibility of a new social orientation in the United States—which will influence the world at large as well—is dependent on what happens to the national informational-cultural condition.

LIBRARY

RING, SUMMER, 1987-88

quarter loans made from the

_____

Due:

Oct 23
Dec 11
Jan 29

Mar 18
Apr 22

June 10
July 15

Aug 26
Oct 21

Notes

Introduction

1. Colin Norman, "Rethinking Technology's Role in Economic Change," *Science*, 240 (May 20, 1988): 977.
2. John Berger, "For Raymond Williams—From 'Who Governs' to 'How to Survive,' " *New Statesman* (March 11, 1988), 28.
3. Vicente Navarro, "The Lincoln Brigade: Some Comments on U.S. History," *Monthly Review* (Sept. 1986), 34.
4. Robert D. Hershey, Jr., "High Joblessness Gaining Acceptance," *New York Times*, Oct. 14, 1986.
5. Peter Waldman, "U.S. Concerns Try Attitudinal Training," *Asian Wall Street Journal*, July 28, 1987.
6. Robert Lindsey, "Spiritual Concepts Drawing a Different Breed of Adherent," *New York Times*, Sept. 29, 1986.

Chapter 1

1. "Reagan Talks to World Bank and I.M.F.," text, *New York Times*, Sept. 30, 1981.
2. William Greider, "Annals of Finance—The Price of Money," *New Yorker* (Nov. 9, 1987), 62. Also William Greider, *Secrets of the Temple: How the Federal Reserve Runs the Country* (New York: Simon & Schuster, 1987).
3. *Harper's Weekly* (Feb. 7, 1874), 122.
4. Walter Lippmann and Charles Merz, "A Test of the News," *New Republic* (Aug. 4, 1920), 1–42.
5. Attorney General A. Mitchell Palmer directed the round-up of 3,500 aliens on Jan. 2 and 5, 1920. These actions became known as "The Palmer Raids."
6. The first "Special Committee on Un-American Activities" was established in March 1937. The second committee under the chairmanship of Congressman Martin Dies was established in May 1938.

7. "U.S. Information and Educational Exchange Act" (Smith-Mundt Act), Jan. 27, 1948; "Immigration and Nationality Act" (McCarran-Walter Act), June 27, 1952; "Labor-Management Relation Act" (Taft-Hartley Act), June 23, 1947.

8. Kenneth Flamm, *Targeting the Computer* (Washington, D.C.: Brookings Institution, 1987).

9. Leslie Gelb, "The Death of the Center," *New York Times,* Sept. 26, 1979.

10. Norman Ornstein, "How To Win in '88: Meld the Unmeldable," *U.S. News and World Report* (Oct. 12, 1987), 33.

11. Herbert I. Schiller and Joseph D. Phillips (eds.), *Super-State: Readings in the Military-Industrial Complex* (Urbana: University of Illinois, 1971).

12. David Dickson, *The New Politics of Science* (New York: Pantheon, 1984).

13. U.S. Department of Commerce, Bureau of the Census, *Statistical Abstract of the United States,* 92nd Annual Edition, 1971, p. 573.

14. William Robbins, "Down on the Superfarm: Bigger Share of Profits," *New York Times,* Aug. 4, 1987.

15. Keith Schneider, "Report Says Biotechnology No Boon to Small Farms," *New York Times,* March 19, 1986.

16. William Serrin, "New Federal Statistics Show Union Membership Has Continued to Decline," *New York Times,* Feb. 8, 1985; Kenneth Noble, "Unions Stage a Recovery in the Public Sector," *New York Times,* Dec. 27, 1987; Henry S. Farber, "The Recent Decline of Unionization in the United States," *Science* 238 (Nov. 13, 1987): 915–20.

17. Leftin Stavrianos, *Greece: American Dilemma or Opportunity* (Chicago: H. Regnery Co., 1952).

18. Harvey A. Levenstein, *Communism, Anticommunism and the CIO* (Westport, CT: Greenwood Press, 1981).

19. William Serrin, "Many Industries Don't Let Strikes Stop Them" *New York Times,* Sept. 30, 1986.

20. Vernon M. Biggs, Jr., "The Growth and Composition of the U.S. Labor Force," *Science* 238 (Oct. 9, 1987): 176–80.

21. Zita Arocha, "U.S. Immigration Nears 80-Year High," *International Herald Tribune,* July 25, 1988.

22. "Tax Burden Is Found to Rise for Poor in U.S.," *New York Times,* Nov. 12, 1987.

23. Ibid.

Chapter 2

1. UNESCO, *Cultural Industries: A Challenge for the Future of Culture* (Paris: 1982), 21.

2. Jeremy Seabrook, *Unemployment* (London: Grenada, 1983), xiii.

3. Thomas Guback, "Capital, Labor Power and the Identity of Film," conference on culture and communication, Temple University, Philadelphia, March 1985.
4. Laura Landro, "Airing Grievances As Cable-TV Industry Keeps Growing, Rivals Demand Reregulation,"*Wall Street Journal*, Sept. 17, 1987.
5. Guback, "Capital."
6. Ellen Graham, "The Children's Hour," *Wall Street Journal*, Jan. 19, 1988.
7. Ben Bagdikian, "The 26 Corporations That Own the Media," *EXTRA!*, the newsletter of F.A.I.R. (Fairness and Accuracy In Reporting), vol. 1, no. 1 (June 1987).
8. Ben H. Bagdikian, *The Media Monopoly* (Boston: Beacon, 1983).
9. "Madison Avenue Is Looking Like Merger Street," *Business Week* (May 12, 1986).
10. Ibid.
11. Bagdikian, *EXTRA!*.
12. Albert Scardino, "USA Today Produces Readers But Not Profits," *New York Times*, July 11, 1988.
13. Karen J. Winkler, "New Approaches Changing the Face of Textbook Publishing," *Chronicle of Higher Education*, vol. XIV, no. 12 (May 16, 1977): 1.
14. Edwin McDowell, "Coaches Help Authors Talk Well to Sell Well," *New York Times*, March 2, 1988. Thomas Whiteside, *The Blockbuster Complex: Conglomerates, Show Business, and Book Publishing* (Middletown, CT: Wesleyan University Press, 1981) provides the "big picture" of conglomeratization in publishing.
15. Aljean Harmetz, "Now Playing: The New Hollywood," *New York Times*, Jan. 10, 1988.
16. Aljean Harmetz, "Movie and TV Writers Go on Strike," *New York Times*, March 8, 1988.
17. Paramount consent decree, May 3, 1948, 334 U.S. 131.
18. Geraldine Fabricant, "2.9 Billion Deal Set for SCI Cable," *New York Times*, Dec. 25, 1987.
19. Aljean Harmetz, "Now Playing."
20. Lester Cole, *Hollywood Red* (Palo Alto: Ramparts Press, 1981).
21. Laura Landro, "Airing Grievances."
22. Geraldine Fabricant, "Is Cable Cornering the Market?" *New York Times*, sec. III, April 17, 1988, p. 1.
23. Andrea Adelson, "Radio Deals Grow Richer in Big Cities," *New York Times*, July 6, 1988.
24. UNESCO, *Cultural Industries*, p. 22 (emphasis added).
25. Franklin D. Roosevelt, first inaugural address, March 4, 1933; Theodore Roosevelt, Aug. 20, 1907. Both quotations in Bohle, *Handbook of American Quotes*.

26. *New York Times,* Jan. 13, 1987.
27. "Freedom Begins at Home," Gannett Corporation advertisement, *New York Times,* June 26, 1979.
28. Richard W. Stevenson, "Times Mirror Plans New Stock Class," *New York Times,* Sept. 4, 1987.
29. Alex S. Jones, "Congress Faces a New Battle Over a 1975 Rule Limiting Media Ownership," *New York Times,* Jan. 11, 1988.
30. I am indebted to Patrice Flichy and Patrick Pajon for this expression.
31. Aljean Harmetz, "Hollywood Hails Lorenz, Documentary Pioneer," *New York Times,* Oct. 21, 1981.
32. Ronald Grover, "Hitching a Ride on Hollywood's Hot Streak," *Business Week* (July 11, 1988), 46–48.
33. Richard Bolton, "Canadian Notes," *Afterimage* (February 1988).
34. Henry Glassie, *Passing the Time in Ballymenone: Culture and History of an Ulster Community* (Philadelphia: University of Pennsylvania Press, 1982).

Chapter 3

1. *Valentine v. Chrestensen,* 316 U.S. 52 (1942).
2. Robert Sherrill, "Hogging the Constitution: Big Business and Its Bill of Rights," *Grand Street* (Fall 1987), 95–114. Years later, Justice Douglas more or less excused this decision as having been " 'casual, almost offhand' and that it had not 'survived reflection.' " Quoted in Lawrence H. Tribe, *American Constitutional Law* (Mineola, N.Y.: The Foundation Press Inc., 1978), 652.
3. Edwin P. Rome and William H. Roberts, *Corporate and Commercial Speech: First Amendment Protection of Expression in Business* (Westport: Quorum, 1985), viii.
4. Mark Tushnet, "Corporations and Free Speech," in David Kairys (ed.), *The Politics of Law: A Progressive Critique* (New York: Pantheon, 1982), 260.
5. Arthur Selwyn Miller, *The Supreme Court and American Capitalism* (New York: The Free Press, 1968). See also, his "On Politics, Democracy and the First Amendment: A Commentary on *First National Bank v. Bellotti,*" *Washington and Lee Law Review,* vol. XXXVIII (1981): 25.
6. Morton Horowitz, *The Transformation of American Law* (Cambridge: Harvard University Press, 1977).
7. *Santa Clara County v. Southern Pacific Railroad,* 118 U.S. 394 (1886).
8. Robert Sherrill, "Hogging the Constitution," p. 108.
9. Howard Zinn, *A People's History of the United States* (New York: Harcourt Brace Jovanovich, 1980), 255.
10. "Intellectual Property," *New York Times,* Aug. 6, 1986.
11. *New York Times,* April 26, 1986.

12. "Oil Company Magazine Makes Friends," *IABC Communication World* (June/July 1986).

13. J. S. Henry, "From Soap to Soapbox: The Corporate Merchandising of Ideas," *Working Papers for a New Society,* vol. VII, no. 3 (May/June 1980): 56.

14. *Virginia Board of Pharmacy v. Citizens Consumer Council,* 425 U.S. 748 (1976).

15. *Bigelow v. Virginia,* 421 U.S. 809 (1975).

16. *Linmark Associates, Inc. v. Willingboro,* 431 U.S. 85 (1977).

17. Ithiel de Sola Pool, *The Technologies of Freedom* (Cambridge: Harvard University Press, 1983), 70.

18. *First National Bank of Boston v. Bellotti,* 435 U.S. (1978).

19. *Consolidated Edison Co. of New York, Inc. v. Public Service Commission of New York,* 447 U.S. 530 (1980).

20. *Central Hudson Gas & Electric Corp. v. Public Service Commission of New York,* 447 U.S. 557 (1980).

21. Rome and Roberts, *Corporate and Commercial Speech,* p. 61.

22. *First National v. Bellotti,* footnote 15, p. 780.

23. Rome and Roberts, *Corporate and Commercial Speech,* p. 61.

24. *New York Times Co. v. Sullivan,* 376 U.S. 254 (1964).

25. Rome and Roberts, *Corporate and Commercial Speech,* p. 203.

26. Steven Shiffrin, "The First Amendment and Economic Regulation: Away from a General Theory of the First Amendment," *Northwestern Law Review,* vol. 78, no. 5 (December 1983): 1224.

27. William Patton and Randall Bartlett, "Corporate 'Persons' and Freedom of Speech: The Political Impact of Legal Mythology," *Wisconsin Law Review,* vol. 1981, no. 3, p. 502.

28. Arthur Selwyn Miller, "On Politics," p. 22.

29. Arthur Selwyn Miller, "On Politics," p. 36.

30. S. Prakash Sethi, "A New War on Corporate 'Propaganda,' " *New York Times,* Aug. 10, 1986.

31. Advertisement by Whittle Communications, *New York Times,* Sept. 14, 1987.

32. Michael DeCourcy Hinds, "TV News Gets a Subtle Sales Pitch As the Press Release Goes Electronic," *New York Times,* April 21, 1987.

33. Ibid.

34. *First National v. Bellotti.*

35. *Virginia Board v. Consumer Council.* The *New York Times* editorially from time to time sounds the same note: "[The Court] recognized commerce as important to American life and facts about services and merchandise valuable information." July 11, 1986.

36. *Preferred Communication, Inc. v. City of Los Angeles, California* 754 *Federal Reporter,* 2nd series, 1985, p. 1396.

37. Mark Mininberg, "Circumstances Within Our Control: Promoting Free-

dom of Expression Through Cable Television," *Hastings Constitutional Law Quarterly,* vol. 11, no. 4 (Summer 1984): 595–96, 598.

38. Frances Seghers, "A Compromise That Could Clear the Airwaves," *Business Week* (July 6, 1987), 28.

39. Steven W. Colford, "High Court's Ruling Sets Back Ad Rights," *Advertising Age* (July 7, 1986), 1.

40. E. R. Shipp, "A.B.A. Rejects Plan on Tobacco Ad Ban," *New York Times,* Feb. 17, 1987.

41. Lena Williams, "Blacks in Debate on Tobacco Industry Influence," *New York Times,* Jan. 17, 1987.

42. Peter Schmeisser, "Pushing Cigarettes Overseas," *New York Times Magazine,* July 10, 1988.

43. John F. Burns, "Canada Passes Law to Ban Tobacco Ads and Curb Smoking," *New York Times,* June 30, 1988.

44. Advertisement in *New York Review of Books,* October 9, 1986; and in *Columbia Journalism Review* (Nov./Dec. 1986).

45. Richard W. Stevenson, "Philip Morris Enlists Pravda in Its Campaign," *New York Times,* Dec. 16, 1987.

46. Richard Levine, "Union's Ad on Smoking Ban Was Paid for by Philip Morris," *New York Times,* Sept. 23, 1987.

47. "Nowhere to Go But Up," *Business Week* (June 29, 1987), 25.

48. Jon Nordheimer, "Ad Tax Defended by Florida Officials," *New York Times,* June 22, 1987.

49. Sidney P. Freedberg, "Fate of Florida's Tax on Services Make Other States Go Slow," *Wall Street Journal,* Sept. 21, 1987.

50. Ibid.; also Michael Schudson, "The Goose and the Golden Eggs," *Gannett Center Journal* (Winter 1988), 119–20.

51. *Posados de Puerto Rico v. Tourism Co.,* no. 84–1903

52. Stuart Taylor, "High Court, 5–4, Sharply Limits Constitutional Protection for Ads," *New York Times,* July 2, 1986.

53. Steven W. Colford, "Rehnquist Cool to Ad Rights," *Advertising Age* (June 23, 1986), 1.

54. Quoted in John S. Saloma III, *Ominous Politics* (New York: Hill & Wang, 1984), 16.

55. Robert Sherrill, "Hogging the Constitution," p. 109.

Chapter 4

1. David Stockman, *The Triumph of Politics: How The Reagan Revolution Failed* (New York: Harper and Row, 1986). Also Daniel Patrick Moynihan, *Came the Revolution* (San Diego: Harcourt Brace Jovanovich, 1988).

2. Burton W. Adkinson, *Two Centuries of Federal Information* (Stroudsberg, PA: Dowden, Hutchinson, and Ross, Inc., 1978).

3. David Dickson, *The New Politics of Science* (New York: Pantheon, 1984).
4. Arthur D. Little, Inc., "Passing the Threshold Into the Information Age: Perspective for Federal Action on Information," basic findings report, prepared for the National Science Foundation, vol. 1, American Library Association, Washington, D.C., Jan. 1978, p. 6.
5. *Science* 239 (February 26, 1988): 965.
6. "Scientific and Technical Information: Options for National Action," prepared by Bruce G. Whalen and Charles C. Joyce, Jr., the Mitre Corporation, Metrek Division, McLean, Virginia, for The National Science Foundation, Division of Science Information, Nov. 1976, p. 3.
7. "Scientific and Technical Information," p. 2.
8. Arthur D. Little, "Passing the Threshold," p. 6.
9. Philip S. Nyborg, Pender M. McCarter, William Erickson (eds.), "Information Processing in the United States: A Quantitative Summary," AFIPS (Montvale, N.J.: undated).
10. "The 1976 Information Year in Review: A Staff Report," *Information Action*, 9:5 (Feb. 1977).
11. U.S. Department of Commerce, *U.S. Industrial Outlook 1986-Information Services* (Jan. 1986), 48.
12. *Information Today*, vol. 5, no. 4 (April 1988), 1.
13. "International Information Flow: A Plan for Action," a statement by Business Roundtable, New York City, Jan. 1985, pp. 6, 11.
14. Lee Burchinal, "Impact of On-Line Systems on National Information Policy and on Local, State and Regional Planning," 1977 Pittsburgh conference on the on-line revolution in libraries, Nov. 14–16, 1977.
15. Anita R. Schiller, "Commercial On-Line Services and the University Library: Some Impacts and Implications," a report to the Council on Library Resources, 1977.
16. Leigh Estabrook, "Productivity, Profit and Libraries," *Library Journal* (July 1981), 1377–81.
17. "Towards a National Program for Library and Information Services: Goals for Action," prepared by the National Commission on Libraries and Information Science, Washington D.C., 1975, p. 17.
18. "Towards a National Program," p. 78.
19. "Towards a National Program," p. 25.
20. "Towards a National Program," p. 24.
21. *National Information Policy,* report to the president of the United States, submitted by the staff of the Domestic Council Committee on the Right of Privacy, published by the National Commission on Libraries and Information Science, Washington, D.C., U.S. Government Printing Office, 1976, pp. 74–75. Emphasis added.
22. *National Information Policy,* p. 76 (first emphasis added, second emphasis in text).

23. *National Information Policy,* p. 81 (emphasis added).

24. Letter, Society for Scholarly Publishing, Jan. 1980, vol. 2, issue 1, ISSN 0193-1938.

25. The White House Conference on Library and Information Services—1979—Summary, March 1980, U.S. Government Printing Office, Washington, D.C., p. 42.

26. White House Conference, resolution on "Pricing of Basic Federal Government Publications," p. 55.

27. *Public Sector/Private Sector Interaction in Providing Information Services,* National Commission on Libraries and Information Science, U.S. Government Printing Office, Washington, D.C., Feb. 1982.

28. Diane Smith, "The Commercialization and Privatization of Government Information," *Government Publications Review,* vol. 12 (1985), 45–63, note p. 57 in particular.

29. *Public Sector/Private Sector Interaction,* p. 33 (emphasis added).

30. Ibid., emphasis added.

31. John Berry, "ALISE in Wonderland," *Library Journal,* vol. 111, no. 5 (March 15, 1986): 4.

32. Roger Summit, *Information Today,* vol. 3, issue 5 (May 1986): 1

33. "Dun & Bradstreet Credit Services Block Labor Unions, Others from Access to Financial Records: Rescind Following National Furor," *Database Searcher,* vol. 3, no. 11 (Dec. 1987).

34. "The Struggle for Public Accountability: OMB Watch in 1987," *OMB Watch* (Jan. 1988), 25.

35. Ann Crittenden, "A World With Fewer Numbers," *New York Times,* July 11, 1982.

36. Ibid.

37. "Nonpartisan Group Finds Fraud in Cook County Voter Rolls," *Boston Globe,* Oct. 24, 1986.

38. American Library Association, "Less Access to Less Information By and About the U.S. Government: IX" (Dec. 1987).

39. Harry Lewis, "Keeping Secrets: Reagan's War on Government Information," *Multinational Monitor* (Sept. 1987), 16–17.

40. "The $3 Billion Question: Whose Info Is It, Anyway?" *Business Week* (July 4, 1988), 106.

41. Jean Evangelauf, "Academe and Business Tighten Ties: Corporate Giving Nears $1.5 Billion," *Chronicle of Higher Education,* vol. xxxi, no. 10 (Nov. 6, 1985): 1

42. Jean Evangelauf, "Line Between Public and Private Institutions Is Blurring in Nations Throughout the World," *Chronicle of Higher Education* (July 1, 1987), 25.

43. Calvin Sims, "Business-Campus Ventures Grow," *New York Times,* Dec. 14, 1987.

44. Nell P. Eurich and Ernest L. Boyer, *Corporate Classrooms: The Learn-*

ing Business (Princeton, N.J.: The Carnegie Foundation for the Advancement of Teaching, 1985), ix, 7–8.

45. Ibid.
46. Leslie Wayne, "Columbia Gives 'F' to a $100,000 Lesson Plan," *New York Times,* Oct. 24, 1987.
47. "Scholarship, Research and Access to Information," a statement from the Council on Library Resources, Washington, D.C., Jan. 1985.

Chapter 5

1. Hans Magnus Enzensberger, *The Consciousness Industry* (New York: The Seabury Press, 1974), esp. Chapter 1, "The Industrialization of the Mind."
2. David E. Nye, *Image Worlds: Corporate Identities at General Electric, 1890–1930* (Cambridge: MIT Press, 1985), 133.
3. Enzensberger, *The Consciousness Industry,* p. 6.
4. Hans Haacke, "Museums, Managers of Consciousness," in *Hans Haacke: Unfinished Business,* (Cambridge: MIT Press, 1987), 71.
5. Brian Wallis, "Institutions Trust Institutions," in *Hans Haacke,* p. 51.
6. Haacke, "Museums, Managers of Consciousness," pp. 152–54.
7. Ibid.
8. *New York Times,* July 2, 1987.
9. *New York Times,* Nov. 13, 1987.
10. *New York Times,* June 18, 1988.
11. *New York Times,* June 21, 1987.
12. Alix M. Freedman, "Blowing Smoke," *Wall Street Journal,* June 8, 1988.
13. Michael Gross, "For Tiffany, 150th Is a Silver Anniversary," *New York Times,* Sept. 15, 1987. Very rich individuals also can obtain the Metropolitan Museum of Art as a background setting for their social affairs. In the spring of 1988, the Met allowed itself to be used as the site for a reception and dinner for 500 guests celebrating the newly wedded offspring of two billionaire families. Georgia Dullea, "Billionaire Families Join in Wall Street Wedding," *New York Times,* April 19, 1988.
14. "Museum Enters the Commercial Age," *New York Times,* Sept. 20, 1987.
15. Brian Wallis, "Institutions Trust Institutions," pp. 52, 54.
16. Hans Haacke, "Museums, Managers of Consciousness," pp. 70–71.
17. Douglas Crimp, *October* 30 (Fall 1984): 6.
18. Deborah Silverman, *Selling Culture* (New York: Pantheon, 1986), 20.
19. Silverman, *Selling Culture,* p. 24.
20. Silverman, *Selling Culture,* p. 31.
21. *Hans Haacke: Unfinished Business,* pp. 98–107.
22. *New York Times,* Nov. 13, 1987.
23. Leo Steinberg, "Some of Hans Haacke's Work Considered As Art," in *Hans Haacke: Unfinished Business,* pp. 8–10.

24. Susan Freudenheim, "Bus Art Scorns City's Smugness," *San Diego Tribune,* Jan. 7, 1988.

25. Kenneth T. Jackson, *Crabgrass Frontier* (New York: Oxford University Press, 1985).

26. William K. Stevens, "Beyond the Mall: Suburbs Evolving into 'Outer Cities,' " *New York Times,* Nov. 8, 1987.

27. Jennifer Stoffel, "What's New in Shopping Malls,"*New York Times,* Aug. 7, 1988.

28. Ellen Graham, "The Pleasure Dome," *Wall Street Journal,* May 13, 1988.

29. Russell Jacoby, *The Last Intellectuals: American Culture in the Age of Academe* (New York: Basic Books, Inc., 1987), 45–46.

30. John Friedmann, "The Right to the City," *Development Dialogue,* 1987:1 (Uppsala, Sweden): 136–137.

31. Judge Sol Wachtler, dissenting opinion, *New York Times,* Dec. 20, 1985.

32. Paul Goldberger, "Plazas, Like Computers, Are Best if User-Friendly," *New York Times,* Nov. 22, 1987.

33. Ada Louise Huxtable, "Creeping Giantism in Manhattan," *New York Times,* March 22, 1987.

34. Michael Rustin, "The Fall and Rise of Public Space," *Dissent* (Fall 1986), 493.

35. Susan G. Davis, *Parades and Power: Street Theatre in Nineteenth Century Philadelphia* (Philadelphia: Temple University Press, 1986), 172–73.

36. Friedmann, "Right to the City," pp. 138–39.

37. Robert Pear, "Judge Citing Commercials, Drops TV Citizenship Oath," *New York Times,* June 28, 1986.

38. Ibid. See also Susan Davis, "Set Your Mood to Patriotic: History as Televised Special Event," *Radical History Review* (Fall 1988).

39. Clyde H. Farnsworth, "Corporations Gear Up for Constitution Party," *New York Times,* Nov. 17, 1986.

40. Barbara Gamarkian, "Now It's a Corporate-Driven Capital Party Circuit," *New York Times,* March 20, 1987.

41. "Chemical Bank Met in the Park," advertisement, *New York Times,* June 19, 1988.

42. "A.T.& T. on Stage," advertisement, *New York Times,* June 5, 1988.

43. Advertisement, *New York Times,* June 5, 1988.

44. "Harlem? Harlem!," advertisement, *New York Times Magazine,* June 26, 1988.

45. J. Peter Grace and Joseph A. Califano, Jr., "Networks vs. Free Press," *New York Times,* June 12, 1986.

46. Benjamin Barber, "What Do 47-Year-Olds Know?" *New York Times,* Dec. 26, 1987.

47. Richard W. Stevenson, "An Industry Turns Volume Up," *New York Times,* Jan. 18, 1986.

48. Warren Weaver, Jr., "Commercial Sponsors Will Claim Equal Time in Presidential Debate," *New York Times,* Dec. 1, 1987.

49. Thomas Morgan, "Is Public TV Becoming Overly Commercial?" *New York Times,* April 9, 1986.

50. *Wall Street Journal,* Oct. 21, 1987.

51. "Kids and TV: Taking Control of the Controls," advertisement, *New York Times,* Nov. 16, 1987.

52. Peter J. Boyer, "House Passes Bill Limiting Commercials in Children's TV," *New York Times,* June 9, 1988.

53. Irvin Molotsky, "Reagan Vetoes Bill Putting Limits on TV Programming for Children," *New York Times,* Nov. 7, 1988.

54. Irvin Molotsky, "2 Broadcast Measures Die in Senate," *New York Times,* Dec. 12, 1987.

Chapter 6

1. Robert B. Horwitz, "Understanding Deregulation," *Theory and Society,* 15: 139–174 (1986): 139.

2. Kevin Kelly, "Going Global, You'll Need Lawyers, Lobbyists and Luck," *Business Week* (March 21, 1988).

3. Dan Schiller, *Telematics and Government* (Norwood, N.J.: Ablex, 1982).

4. Colleen Roach, "The U.S. Position on the New World Information and Communication Order," *Journal of Communication,* vol. 37, no. 4 (Autumn 1987): 36–38.

5. Ibid.

6. Paul Lewis, "U.S. Lessens Presence at Third World Forum," *New York Times,* July 9, 1987.

7. Paul Lewis, "Linking of Arms Cuts to Aid Rejected," *New York Times,* Sept. 11, 1987.

8. Steven Greenhouse, "The Global March to Free Markets," *New York Times,* July 19, 1987.

9. James Brooke, "In Africa, A Rush to Privatize," *New York Times,* July 30, 1987 and March 14, 1988.

10. Paul Lewis, "West to Resume Farm Aid to Ethiopia," *New York Times,* Feb. 6, 1988.

11. "International Information Flows: A Plan for Action," a statement by the Business Roundtable, Jan. 1985, p. 3.

12. "International Information Flows," p. 17.

13. "International Information Flows," p. 6.

14. "Tall Orders," *New York Times,* Jan. 24, 1988.

15. Stanley Meisler, "Mulroney Wins in Canada, Saving U.S. Trade Pact," *Los Angeles Times,* Nov. 22, 1988.

16. "From Now to the Twenty-First Century," a pamphlet by the Global

Media Commission, International Advertising Association, undated, probably mid-1985.

17. Ibid.

18. "The Media Barons Battle to Dominate Europe," *Business Week* (May 25, 1987).

19. "U.S. Television Sets Sights on Europe's Expanding Industry," *International Herald Tribune,* July 23–24, 1988.

20. Roger Watkins, "Europe Is Facing Commercial TV," *Variety's 17th International Television Annual* (April 23, 1986), 1.

21. "U.S. Television Sets Sights."

22. "Media Barons."

23. Peter Fiddick, "Murdoch Launches a War in the Air," *Guardian,* June 9, 1988.

24. "Mogul's Gamble," *Wall Street Journal,* Aug. 9, 1988.

25. "Media Barons."

26. Harry Jaffe, "The Emperor's New Woes," *Channels* (Oct. 1986), 64.

27. *New York Times,* Dec. 13, 1987.

28. John Tagliabue, "Poland Bids Benvenuto to Italian TV," *New York Times,* April 3, 1988.

29. UNESCO, World Conference on Cultural Policies, July 26–Aug. 6, 1982, final report.

30. Leslie Bennetts, "French Culture Minister Finds Empathy in U.S.," *New York Times,* Oct. 29, 1986.

31. Douglas C. McGill, "Louvre Seeks Financing to Expand Its Activities," *New York Times,* July 11, 1987.

32. Leslie Bennetts, "French Culture Minister."

33. Thomas Kamm, "French TV Embroiled in a Bidding War," *Wall Street Journal,* May 27, 1987, quoting Jean-Marie Canada, managing director of Antenne 2, the state-owned channel.

34. Ibid.

35. James M. Markham, "Paris Journal: Off-Screen TV: Scandal, Sex, Money," *New York Times,* Jan. 18, 1988.

36. Henry Giniger, "J. R. Ewing and Captain Furillo in Paris," *New York Times,* Nov. 21, 1987.

37. Ibid.

38. "Rupert Murdoch's Big Move" *Business Week* (May 20, 1985).

39. Jay Sharbutt, "American Networks Seek Global Audience for U.S. TV Newscasts," *Los Angeles Times,* Jan. 4, 1988.

40. Patrick J. Leahy, "How to Protect © in World Markets," *New York Times,* April 21, 1988.

41. Richard W. Stevenson, "TV Boom in Europe Aids U.S. Producers," *New York Times,* Dec. 28, 1987.

42. Richard W. Stevenson, "Bringing Hollywood Hits to China's Movie Goers," *New York Times,* Dec. 27, 1987.

43. William A. Honan, "House Unit Backs Bill on Copyright Pact," *New York Times,* April 28, 1988.

44. William J. Holstein and Amy Borrus, "Japan's Clout in the U.S.," *Business Week* (July 11, 1988).

45. Ira Berkow, "The Superbowl Strut," *New York Times,* Feb. 1, 1988.

46. "Nothing Sells Like Sports," *Business Week* (Aug. 31, 1987).

47. "Will Corporate Sponsors Get Burned by the Torch?" *Business Week* (Feb. 1, 1988).

48. Michael Janofsky, "U.S. Soccer Officials Say World Cup Would Revive Game," *New York Times,* July 4, 1988.

49. "Nothing Sells Like Sports," *Business Week* (Aug. 31, 1987).

50. John Holusha, "A New Fast Lane for Business," *New York Times,* June 19, 1987.

51. Don A. Schance, "Politics, American Style: Italians Seek Media Image," *Los Angeles Times,* May 28, 1987.

52. "The Selling of European Politicians, American-Style," *Business Week* (July 7, 1986), 26–28.

53. Ibid.

54. "Global Marketing," p. 18.

55. "Global Marketing," p. 24.

56. Ibid.

57. Terese P. Sevigny, UN Under-Secretary General for Public Information, address to the Eleventh Public Relations World Congress, Melbourne, Australia, April 28, 1988.

58. *New York Times,* Feb. 16, 1986.

59. Patrick McDonnell, "MexFest Bash: Rock Rolls Crowd Across the Border," *Los Angeles Times,* July 1, 1987.

60. Ngugi wa Thiong'o, *Decolonising The Mind* (London: James Currey, 1986), 3.

Chapter 7

1. Elihu Katz, "On Conceptualizing Media Effects," *Studies in Communication,* vol. 1 (1980): 119–41. Elihu Katz, "Communications Research Since Lazarsfeld," *Public Opinion Quarterly,* vol. 51, no. 4, part 2 (Winter 1987): S-25–S-45.

2. Ibid.

3. Daniel Lerner, "Communication and Development," in Daniel Lerner and Lyle M. Nelson, *Communication Research—A Half Century Appraisal* (Honolulu: University of Hawaii Press, 1977), 148.

4. "Point IV," *Fortune* (February 1950), 89.

5. Lerner, "Communication and Development."

6. Ibid., emphasis added.

7. Warren R. Reid (ed.), *Public Papers of the Presidents,* vol. 19 (Washington, D.C.: General Services Administration, 1964), 112–16.

8. Daniel Lerner, "Managing Communication for Modernization: A Development Construct," in Arnold A. Rogow (ed.), *Politics, Personality and Social Science in the Twentieth Century: Essays in Honor of Harold D. Lasswell* (Chicago: University of Chicago Press, 1969), 182 (emphasis added).

9. Daniel Lerner, "Communication and Development," p. 182.

10. D. Lerner, "Communication and Development," p. 183 (emphasis in text, translation by D. Lerner).

11. A. W. Singham and Tran Van Dinh, *From Bandung to Colombo: Conferences of the Non-Aligned Countries, 1955–1975* (New York: Third Press Review, 1976), 161.

12. Elihu Katz, "On Conceptualizing Media Effects," p. 130.

13. William Harley, *Journal of Communication,* vol. 34, no. 4 (Autumn 1984): 84.

14. "From Now to the Twenty-First Century," a pamphlet by the Global Media Commission, The International Advertising Association, undated, probably mid-1985.

15. Martha Rosler, " 'Video Art,' Its Audience, Its Public," *Independent* (Dec. 1987), 16.

16. Ithiel de Sola Pool, *The Technologies of Freedom* (Cambridge: Harvard University Press, 1983).

17. James G. Webster, *Journal of Communication,* vol. 36, no. 3 (Summer 1986): 78.

18. Webster, *Journal of Communication,* p. 89.

19. Richard W. Stevenson, "The Networks and Advertisers Try to Recapture Our Attention," *New York Times,* Oct. 20, 1985.

20. Sally Bedell Smith, "New TV Technologies Are Starting to Change the Nation's Viewing Habits," *New York Times,* Oct. 9, 1985.

21. Elihu Katz and Tamar Liebes, "Mutual Aid In The Reading of Dallas: Preliminary Notes From A Cross-Cultural Study," in Philip Drummond and Richard Patterson (eds.), *Television in Transition* (London: British Film Institute, 1986), 187–98.

22. Thomas L. Friedman, "J. R.'s Message? As Varied As Kibbutz and Bazaar." *New York Times,* April 1, 1985.

23. Ibid.

24. Ien Ang, *Watching Dallas* (New York: Methuen, 1985).

25. Ang, *Watching Dallas,* p. 10.

26. Robyn Penman, "Issues In International Communications: Implications For the International Year of Peace," paper presented to the Canberra Conference on International Communication, Dec. 1–5, 1986, Canberra, Australia.

27. Michael Tracy, "The Poisoned Chalice: International Television and Idea of Dominance," *Daedalus,* vol. 114, no. 4 (Fall 1985): 41.

28. Tracy, "The Poisoned Chalice," *Daedalus,* p. 45. Also "Popular Culture and the Economics of Global Television," *Intermedia,* vol. 16, no. 2 (March 1988): 9–25.

29. Philip Schlesinger, "On National Identity: Some Conceptions and Misconceptions Criticized," in *Social Science Information* 2 (1987): 232.

30. John Fiske and John Hartley, *Reading Television* (London: Methuen, 1977), 108.

31. Fiske and Hartley, *Reading Television,* p. 102 (emphasis in text).

32. Elayne Rapping, *The Looking Glass World of Non-Fiction TV* (Boston: South End Press, 1987), 18.

33. J. Fred MacDonald, *Television and the Red Menace: The Video Road to Vietnam* (New York: Praeger, 1985).

34. Wiliam Atwood, *The Twilight Struggle* (New York: Harper & Row, 1987). Also Lloyd Garrison's review of this book in *New York Times Book Review,* Aug. 30, 1987, p. 12.

35. Alan Tonnelson review of Thomas G. Paterson, *Meeting the Communist Threat: Truman to Reagan* in the *New York Times Book Review,* May 29, 1988, p. 16.

Chapter 8

1. Felix Rohatyn, "Restoring American Independence," *New York Review of Books,* Feb. 18, 1988, p. 8.

2. Stephen S. Cohen and John Sysman, *Manufacturing Matters: The Myth of the Post-Industrial Society* (New York: Basic Books, 1987).

3. "Glutted Markets," *Wall Street Journal,* March 9, 1987.

4. Winston Williams, "Waking Up to the Glut Economy," *New York Times,* Sec. 3, Dec. 8, 1987.

5. Athan G. Theoharis and John Stuart Cox, *The Boss: J. Edgar Hoover and the Great American Inquisition* (Philadelphia: Temple University Press, 1988).

6. Ben Bagdikian, *The Media Monopoly,* revised edition (Boston: Beacon Press, 1987).

7. Draft of bishops' letter on the U.S. economy, *New York Times,* Nov. 12, 1984.

8. Kenneth A. Briggs, "Catholic Group Extols Capitalism As Bishops Ready Study," *New York Times,* Nov. 7, 1984.

9. John Shattuck and Muriel Morisey Spence, "Government Information Controls: Implications for Scholarship, Science and Technology," Association of American Universities, Washington, D.C., March 31, 1988.

10. *New York Times,* Nov. 1, 1987.

Index

ABC (American Broadcasting Corporation), 36
Abuses: in the corporate system, 19; in government, 19, 161–62
Academia, 20, 21n, 24, 67, 86–87, 129, 146, 167, 171–72
Access: to channels, 57, 147, 148; to cultural industries, 32; to education, 4; to information, 54, 69–70, 88, 165; to libraries, 4, 68–69, 75, 78–79, 86; to the media, 49, 50–51, 120–23, 132; to shopping malls, 100–103
Accountability, 12, 19, 47, 56–57, 63, 112, 137n, 144–45, 171, 172
Action for Children's Television, 108
Active audience, 146–49, 151–54
Advertising: advocacy, 54–55; of casino gambling, 63; and children's television, 59; constitutional protection for, 4, 50–53, 55–56, 60–63; and consumerism, 166; and deregulation, 123–24; dissatisfaction with, 59; effectiveness of, 4; in Europe, 123–24; as an example of corporate speech, 121; expenditures for, 124; in Florida, 62–63; and the free-press doctrine, 167; and the global market, 57, 124, 130, 132–34, 141; and the ideology of freedom, 166; and mergers/monopolies, 35–36, 164; and national broadcasting systems, 121–22; and national sovereignty, 133; and newspapers, 36; and noncommercial broadcasting, 121; as ritualistic, 4; for social goals, 50–51; and sports events, 130; as a supportive activity of the cultural industries, 34; taxes on, 62–63, 165; and technological develop-

ment, 122–23; on television, 107; tobacco, 60–62; and transnational corporations, 35–36, 121, 123–24, 128–29
Advocacy advertising, 54–55
Aestheticism, 159–60
Africa, 128, 134, 137
Agenda setting, 24–25, 143, 168–69
Agriculture/farming, 14, 21–22
Aid to other countries, U.S., 115–17, 138–39, 144–45, 155
Airwaves, 106–10
Alfred A. Knopf, 37
Algiers conference (UNESCO, 1973), 142
Alternative media, 143, 167–68
American Bar Association, 60
American Enterprise Institute, 129
American Federation of Information Processing Societies (AFIPS), 71–72
American Library Association, 78
American Museum of Natural History, 94
American Television and Communication Corporation, 39
Amerman, David P., 37
Ang, Ien, 150
Annenberg media interests, 124
Anticommunism, 14–19, 20, 23–25, 139, 155–56, 162
Antilabor campaign, 25, 39
Art galleries. *See* Museums; *name of specific gallery*
Arthur D. Little Report (1978), 70
Arts/artists, 39, 40, 43, 92–93, 159, 172–73
Asia, 128, 134, 137
Associated Press, 141